Master Your Emotions

ROBERT W. GILL

Contents

Intorduction

Our feelings or emotions are a major part of our inner lives. Our emotions are sometimes rapid primitive reflexes independent of our thoughts, but at other times, our feelings reflect our cognitive assessment of our current situation. Our feelings involve both our emotions and our urges to act certain ways. Thus, emotions determine if we are happy or unhappy, if we want to approach something or run away from it, if we are exuberant or frozen, etc.

Emotions are frequently unrealistic and irrational, i.e. unreasonable, unthinking automatic physiological reactions or based on faulty ideas distorted by our past experiences, misperceptions, exaggerated fears or hopes or needs. Examples: Reason usually doesn't over-ride subjective experience, i.e. telling a person afraid of spiders that this specific spider right here is completely harmless, doesn't completely reduce his/her fear. The intensity of an emotion is not so much determined by the current situation as it is by the amount of actual or expected change. Thus, a small spider seen 15 feet away (a small change) is not as scary as a large one suddenly only 6 inches away. Likewise, if economic conditions in the 1990's changed radically and returned to 1935 standards, our national feelings of crisis would be much greater than they were during the middle of the Great Depression. Where the change is greatest, the feelings are most intense. It was the wealthy and ambitious who committed suicide in 1929, not the poor. The college graduate who always wanted and expected to become a doctor is more crushed by rejection letters from Medical School than the graduate who rather expected the rejections.

Since emotions seem to be designed by nature to help us adapt, to solve problems, we tend to get "used to" positive conditions (a loving, giving spouse) but our fears and hostilities continue on and on upsetting and urging us to "do something." The human mind was apparently not made for happiness, but for survival. Happiness is possible, but it may take intentional thought and effort; it is not always an automatic process.

But anger, grief, insecurity, and jealousy are automatic, sometimes even unstoppable.

The desire to remove serious emotional hurts from our life can become so primary that our strong feelings override reason, close our minds to other viewpoints, and dominate our actions. Suicide is a way to escape pain and hurts. Likewise, the enraged ex-spouse can hardly think of anything else, certainly not any explanations for the former spouse's wrongdoings. The badness of the ex-spouse becomes an obsession, an unshakeable conviction which will often last forever, regardless of other peoples' opinions. This single- minded view is a characteristic of emotions: the fearful flyer cannot consider the high probability of his/her flight arriving safely; the jealous person is absolutely certain the lover is interested in someone else; the insecure spouse feels sure his/her partner doesn't really care for him/her. Yet, there sometimes seems to be a consideration of the probable consequences at some semi-conscious level because the fearful passenger usually doesn't get off the plane and we don't always immediately dump the "unfaithful" lover or "indifferent" spouse. Indeed, many "healthy" people tend to distort their view of a situation in such a way that their negative feelings and dangers are minimized and/or their positive feelings are maximized. Fortunately, under favorable conditions, reason can help us see other possibilities, see the likely long-term consequences of an action. Reason (cognition) can modify the impulsive actions of the more rigidly mechanistic emotions.

Emotions, as well as behavior and reason, are lawful and understandable (but not logical). The more you know about those laws, the better your chances of controlling your unwanted emotions. Learning to control our emotions We are probably always feeling emotions; they seem to impose themselves on us; we ordinarily don't "will" to feel certain ways. The range of emotions is extensive. We can feel terrible, as in horror, suicidal depression, rage, and self-depreciation. Even in milder forms, such as tension or boredom or irritation or subordination, emotions may make us miserable. Yet, we can feel happy, proud, loving, or fascinated, which makes life great. At this point in time, psychologists know more about reducing unwanted feelings than about increasing the desired emotions. This book focuses on methods for controlling our emotions, primarily anxiety, depression, anger, and passive-dependency.

Stay within your limitations and stay centered to stay on course. Too often we allow our emotions to control and dictate the scope and outcome of our lives. Our emotions sometimes tend to get out in front of us when we need to control the pace and purpose of our lives in order to realize and release our full potential.

A good technique to learn in order to master your emotions is to be responsive, not reactive. To be reactive is to respond to a situation or comment without thinking through how you really feel about it. On the other hand, to be responsive implies taking the time to process and come to terms with how you view or experience the situation. When confronted with an emotionally charged situation, try counting to 10 before offering a response.

There is a big difference between living with emotions and being emotionally. Emotions are essential for personal development and to maintain intimate relationships. Passion, love, and excitement are all examples of healthy emotions. Feeling these emotions will help you to live to your full potential. For example, if you "live" passion each day to be the person you want to be, you will be far more successful in your journey.

Alternately, if you allow your emotions to control your happiness and sense of purpose, you will not be as productive. The reason for this is simple and quite clear. You must stay focused on what you what and how you are going about getting what you want as a matter of habit. You must control how you feel and then channel these feelings, these emotions, into productive progress. Remember to live life as a marathon race - not a sprint.

Being emotional is similar to being a victim - you are allowing your emotions to dictate what you do and how you are feeling. The bottom line, and the really good news, is you are in control of how you respond and master your emotions. You have the power, right now, to decide to be a person of choice.

Chapter One

How To Regain Emotional Control

The Power of Your Emotions

Emotions are incredibly powerful forces. They are able to propel you to achieve your destiny and overcome the most traumatic events, or they can cause you to become immobilized by small setbacks. Life will always present you with surprises, and you can only exert so much control over the world outside you. However, you always-always-have the choice to manage and balance your emotions. It may not seem this way when your strong emotions get the better of you, but you don't have to be at their mercy. You also needn't remain in unhappy situations, unable to move forward because you're convinced that you don't have enough enthusiasm, courage, or determination to get out of your rut and onto the path of your destiny.

It's important to realize that there's no way you can have complete control over your emotions. Everyone has off days, and we all suffer the traumas that are a natural part of life. People die or move away, relationships come to an end, and disappointments occur. There will be times when you experience negative feelings, such as anger or sadness, as well as occasions when your positive ones, including confidence or happiness, aren't as strong as you'd like them to be. Yet when you've developed your ability to balance your emotions, unexpected problems won't knock you off balance as easily, and you'll return more quickly to a positive outlook.

Balanced Emotions

When your emotions are in balance, you probably don't give them much thought. Whatever your situation, you're feeling good. You want to do considerate things and be kind to other people because you're in touch with your highest self and filled with love. You're optimistic about the future, and you aren't looking back at the past with regret. You're content and peaceful, accepting things just the way they are, yet you're also energetic and enthusiastic. When you don't feel this way, you could think that it's because life has gone awry, but that's not the case. You may miss your exit on the freeway and spend an unexpected 20 minutes doubling back, or you might open your credit-card bill and discover that you've gone way over budget this month, but neither of these experiences has to result in your becoming furious, completely stressed out, or terrified. You do have a choice about the way you feel, as well as how much fear you experience (as opposed to confidence) and your level of joy in relation to sadness.

I've found that when my emotions are in balance, I feel a deep sense of gratitude. I recognize the gifts I have and everything that's wonderful in my life, and I put any problems that I'm experiencing into perspective. I feel compelled to contribute to the world, and my mind becomes filled with positive thoughts. However, when my emotions are out of balance, I focus on what isn't working in my life instead of what is.

Emotions, Thoughts, And Behaviors

Thoughts, feelings, and behaviors all influence each other, but the strongest force is our emotions-and that's why it's so important to take control of, and balance, them. While we may act or think obsessively, we only do so when our behavior or thoughts are driven by strong emotions. For instance, if people are addicted to alcohol, they reach for that glass of wine or vodka again and again because when they drink, they stimulate the pleasure centers in their brain and experience a false sensation of joy, well-being, calm, or confidence. While alcoholics may be determined not to drink and to never think about doing so-and might even clear out their liquor cabinet so that they can't pour themselves a stiff one-their strong desire to feel the emotions that drinking creates for them may overrule their attempts to control their thoughts and behaviors.

In the same way, if we obsessively think about something, it's because strong emotions are driving our thoughts. When we're facing a challenge and we're trying to think through our options, if our feelings aren't overwhelming us, we can readily become distracted, finding it easy to pull our attention away from the subject for a while. Thoughts such as I wonder what would happen if I approached the situation from this perspective? might pop up while we're in the shower or walking through the grocery store, and we'll go into a creative mode as we think, but we don't get upset or obsessive. However, when a strong emotion is driving our thoughts, it's much harder to shake them. Suddenly, we have insomnia as we spend the early-morning hours fearfully reflecting on what might happen to us, or we endlessly reminisce about a former romantic partner because we're caught up in grief. It's our emotions that trap us in obsessive thoughts.

Emotions! It seems that you're never without them. Oh, sometimes they're quiet, not particularly bothering you, but somehow you know they're there, lurking in the background, just waiting for something to happen. And when it does, WHAM! You feel mad, you feel sad, you feel bad, and you just don't know what to do. All of your thoughts, attitudes and feelings are colored by your emotions. The job or career you have, the kind of person you marry, how you get along with people, every area of your life is influenced by your emotions. In fact, your success or failure in life is actually determined by how well you're able to deal with your negative feelings. Unfortunately, most people try to ignore their negative feelings, rather than deal with them, because they don't quite know how to handle them. Often, you'll try to suppress the feelings... push them down into the subconscious so you can forget that you have them.

If that doesn't work and you're still reeling under the attack, you might try the escape route... drugs, alcohol, sex, quit the job, leave the person, move to another town. Or you might try to talk yourself into feeling better. But sometimes you can't do those things, so, the only thing left is to express the feelings... cry your eyes out, shout at people, punch them in the nose. Right? Wrong! You can get rid of your negative emotions, and the best part is that it can be easy and it's fun. The first step is to get a good look at your negative emotions, rather than hiding your head in the sand.

It's important to realize that you are unique. The decisions you've made about the way the world is and how you should behave in it evolved through your own special combination of birth, upbringing, circumstances of life and, most importantly, your reaction to things you've been told.

In brief, your belief system. However, the things you were told may not have been correct, and decisions you made when you were a child do not often serve you well as an adult. In addition, they result in a lot of misunderstanding, guilt and pain, and prevent your natural beauty from shining through. So, it's important to become aware of the negative elements which are no longer helpful, and get rid of them.

Emotional mastery is the key to living a life that you direct. The ability to have absolute direct power over what you feel in every single moment—no matter what happens around you—is one of the most important skill sets you can have.

Whatever you feel, you're not feeling it because you have to feel it. You're feeling it because you've chosen to feel it. In order to master your emotions and consciously choose the emotions you want to live in, you need to understand these three forces and how to use them to your advantage.

There are three forces in the world that determine what you feel. Together, these three patterns create any—and every—emotional state.

1. Physiology

Emotion is created by motion. Whatever you're feeling right now is directly related to how you're using your body. If you slump your shoulders and lean your head forward, you'll move toward a state of depression. However, the next time you find yourself in a negative state, stand up, throw your shoulders back and take a few deep breaths. You'll find that you're able to put yourself in a resourceful state. From this state, you can make stronger decisions and enjoy a sense of certainty that will keep you calm in the face of uncertainty.

2. Language

Language comes in many forms, one of which includes the questions you ask yourself, either aloud or inside your head. If you ask, "Why does this always have to happen to me?" you'll create a much different set of emotions than if you asked, "How can I benefit from this?" or "Where's the gift in this?" or "What's humorous about this?"

The language patterns you run play a significant role in the meaning you give a situation—and the emotion that situation creates in you. When you feel negative emotions taking over, look at the language surrounding your situation. How can you shift it to create a more empowering state?

3. Focus

Where focus goes, energy flows. And where energy flows, whatever you're focusing on grows. In other words, your life is controlled by what you focus on. That's why you need to focus on where you want to go, not on what you fear. When you next find yourself in a state of uncertainty, resist your fear. Shift your focus toward where you want to go and your actions will take you in that direction.

When you can influence your emotions, you can choose to spend more time in positive, resourceful emotional states. From these states, you'll make the decisions that will help you reach your highest potential and enjoy your life in every moment.

Many persons feel that their emotions are not in their control. They believe that they are slaves to their emotions and that they are just reacting to the events of their lives. There are even those who fear their emotions as if it is some great big tyrant. In an effort to avoid feeling certain emotions many people do things like turn to drugs, alcohol, overeating, sex and even get into a paralyzing depression.

Most of us handle emotions in four common ways:

Denial.

We all use this strategy at some point. It generally it occurs when we try to disassociate from our feelings by saying things like " it really doesn't hurt that bad" Yet we keep holding on to how terrible things are, or how no matter what we do and how perfect we do them, things will always turn out wrong, and why does this always happen to us. If you have done this, what you are doing is focusing on the wrong thing by the disempowering questions you keep asking yourself. You see when you experience an emotion and then try to pretend it's not there you create more pain for yourself. So by ignoring the signals your emotions are trying to send you, you will never be able to make things better. If you ignore these signals the emotions will only just increase their intensity and will keep intensifying until you finally decide to attend to it.

Avoidance

This is another approach we all use as we try to avoid those painful emotions we experience. As we do this we also tend to avoid any situation that may lead to the emotions we that fear. So if you fear being criticized, then you would try to avoid any situations that would lead to you being criticized. You will shy away from certain relationships or even from applying for certain challenging jobs. When you deal with emotion in this manner you are setting yourself up for a big trap, because although avoiding negative situation may protect you in the short-term, it keeps you from feeling the sense of achievement, being praised and the approval and success you desire most. Ultimately what you'll learn is that you can't avoid feeling.

Indulgence

Many of us tend to get to a point where we stop fighting our painful emotions and decide to just totally indulge in them. We submerge ourselves in them so deep that instead of learning the positive messages our emotions are trying to give us, we make it so intense that we end up making it worse. We then begin to say things like "if you think things are hard for you, let me tell you how hard it is for me" It's as if the emotion become an integral part of who we are and what makes us unique. We then begin to take pride in being worse off than anyone else. This approach tends to end up becoming a self-fulfilling prophecy with the person having a vested interest in feeling bad all the time and that's when they are truly trapped.

If you want you life to work, it's imperative that you make your emotions work for you. Do not run or hide from them, do not fool yourself about them or what they mean and never allow them to run or control your life. Your emotions whether positive or negative are like a map with directions pointing you towards the actions you need to take to get to your desired goal.

You must comprehend the truism, that your emotions are there to serve you and until you see that, you can never effectively use your emotions. To create the results you desire for a higher quality of life, you must learn from your emotions and in turn use them to that end. Your negative emotions therefore are really a call to action, a signal that something needs to be done. The moment you begin to be familiar with signals your emotions are sending you and the messages there in, your emotions will also begin to aid you. You will be guided through highs and lows of this life and once you learn to use these signals you'll begin to have the confidence to experience all the wealth you are capable of. It is therefore necessary to master your emotions and use them to your advantage

How To Master Your Emotions.

The first thing you need to do when mastering your emotions is to know your true feelings. Have you ever felt so overwhelmed that you don't even know what you're truly feeling? All you know is that negative emotions and feelings seem to be swarming through you. Interrupt this pattern by stepping back for a moment and just ask yourself "What am I truly feeling at this moment?" if your fist thought is that "I'm frustrated" ask yourself right away "Am I truly frustrated or is it something else?" "Could it be that what I am feeling is disappointment?" By simply taking a moment to figure out what you are truly feeling and questioning and challenging your emotions you will be able to lessen the intensity of the emotion you're experiencing and hence be able to deal with the situation much quicker. You'll also find it easier to learn from the emotion.

Next you must admit and give value to your emotions, because they anchor you. Many of us have had those moments when we make our emotions wrong. This is something you should never do, as it is a sure way of blocking true communication with your inner self and even with other persons. What you must do is be grateful and thankful that your brain is sending you signals of support urging you to take action to change your perceptions or something in your life even your present actions. By trusting your emotions even when you don't understand them and knowing that they are there to support you in making positive changes, you will begin to end the internal wars you have with yourself. You'll then begin to seek out and move towards the simpler solutions.

You then have to be eager to learn what your emotions are saying to you. Do not just accept your emotions on face value, for sometimes what you presently feel is really about something else. When you become eager to learn what your emotions are saying to you, you will begin to master them, which in turn assists you in solving the challenge and prevent the said problem from reoccurring. So if you find yourself feeling rejected, for example, ask yourself "could I be misinterpreting the situation to mean I'm not good enough, when in reality I am using one instance to make my determination?" "What if I approached other persons who may be accepting of me?" "Is my feeling rejected a message that I need to take action to change how I present myself? Ask yourself the following four questions when questioning what your emotions are saying to you:

1. What is it that I truly want to feel?

2. To feel the way I have been feeling what would I have to believe?

3. To create a solution and handle this right now what am I willing to do?

4. Is there anything I can learn from this?

5. What actions can I take now?

You answers to these questions will help you to learn about your emotions and their uniqueness each time they occur.

It's very important that you believe you can do it, that you can deal with this emotion right now. The simplest, most powerful and quickest way to handle an emotion is to recall an instance in the past when you felt a similar emotion and recognize that you had successfully handled it before. If you dealt with it in the past then it is possible that you can deal with it again right now. Think about how you dealt with your emotions in the past and use this as your guide for what you can do right now to change how you feel. What was your process back then? Did you change your perception, what you focused on, and the questions you asked yourself? Do the same things right now believing that it will work just as it did before. So if you're feeling lonely, for example, and you were able to turn it around in the past, ask yourself "What did I do back then?" Did you take action by calling up some of your friends and staying in touch with them thereafter? Did you visit your friends at their home? Whatever you did in the past try them out right now and you will likely get similar results.

Next you have to be sure you can handle the emotion in the future. To do this you need a great plan to do so. One method you can use is to remember the way you have handled it in the past and rehearse handling those situations where this negative emotion would come up in the future. You will have to use visualization to hear, feel and see yourself handling the situation with ease. By doing this over and over again with some emotional intensity will cause your behavior to be set in such a way you will easily deal with the challenge. You can also write down a couple of other ways (at least four of them) you can change your perceptions when negative emotions arises. Do this also for ways you can change how you communicate your feelings and your needs and also for ways you could change the actions you were taking in this particular situation.

The next step is to take action. It makes no sense to go through the first five steps and not take immediate action, you would have wasted your time and nothing would have changed. So once you believe you can handle an emotion take action immediately to prove to yourself that you can handle it.

Emotional Reactions

Many basic emotional reactions may not be learned; they may be inborn physiological responses, like pain, fear, crying, hunger, sensual and sexual pleasure, frustration, pleasure, etc. These and other emotions, like ecstasy, sadness, irritability, rebelliousness, fears, or sudden episodes of agoraphobia, may be genetic, physiological, hormonal or drug-induced and responsive to medication. As we grow out of early childhood, however, certain emotions become associated with certain situations and events; that is a learning process. Many of these associations are not rational. We fear situations that are not dangerous (like meeting someone or speaking up in class). We get upset about things that couldn't be avoided. We may briefly distrust the entire opposite male or female sex after we have been dumped by one of them.

Understanding the way we acquired a certain complex emotional reaction might help us figure out how to change the feeling. On the other hand, knowing the etiology of each emotion may not be necessary. It seems quite likely that several treatment methods will work regardless of the causes.

Are Feelings Good Or Bad?

A common saying is "you are responsible for your feelings." (For the moment, let's forget about reflexive and unconscious feelings.) Fortunately, all feelings can be viewed as natural, as neither good nor bad. This is how: many people believe that feelings and thoughts cannot be bad because they hurt no one. Acts can be bad (because they can hurt). From this viewpoint, there would be no need to hide our feelings (unless disclosing the feelings hurt someone) and no need to feel guilty about any thoughts or feelings.

However, it is easy to see how we come to believe that thoughts and feelings are bad. Suppose as a child you hit your little brother and were spanked and told, "don't do that." As a 5-year-old you aren't likely to figure out that the parent who hit you meant "your hitting is bad but feeling angry is OK," so you grow up thinking "feeling angry is bad." Many of our feelings are suppressed by being told "don't be a scaredy cat," "big kids don't cry," "touching yourself down there is naughty," etc. So, we learn to deny or dislike or feel guilty about many feelings. We even hide many positive feelings: "I don't want him/her to know I like him/her because he/she might not like me."

Feelings usually find a way to express themselves, however. There are several ways subjective feelings get expressed:

1. You may act on feelings: shout at someone when angry, cry when sad, communicate (in body language) your interest when attracted to someone. (These same behaviors--shouting, crying and attracting--surely influence our feelings too.)

2. You may have physiological reactions when feeling something: you blush when embarrassed, have high blood pressure when anxious, sexual arousal when attracted. Actually, psychologists do not yet know whether arousal precedes, accompanies, or follows an emotional reaction.

3. You may try to suppress the feelings and deny being upset or angry. Quite often people who deny their emotions think they are healthy and well adjusted, but they tend to have high blood pressure, high heart rate, an immune deficiency, high incidence of cancer, difficulty sleeping, and lots of aches and pains.

4. You may try to change the situation: shout out orders like a drill sergeant when things go wrong or become charming to attract and influence someone. Note: yelling "shut up" at someone implies but doesn't directly express your feeling, "I'm angry at you."

5. You may have one feeling to deny or conceal another: criticism may hide attraction, crying may occur when you are mad, love may hide scared dependency. Or, you

may have one feeling in response to another feeling: disgust to your own homosexual interests, frustration to your shyness.

6. You may blame others rather than assuming responsibility for your own feelings: "You are a selfish, mean person" instead of "I feel very hurt," "You are a lazy slob" instead of "I feel furious when you are so sloppy," "You are arrogant" instead of "I'm afraid you won't like me." Remember: you are more responsible than anyone else for your feelings. In general, no one can make you feel any way; it is usually your choice (although some emotions are impossible to control--like a startle reaction or grief following the loss of a loved one).

7. You may not be aware of the true nature of your emotions but they can still have an effect on your life. Dramatic examples are people with multiple personalities; an unconscious personality may have feelings which are not known to the person until that personality becomes conscious and "in control" later. Another rare example is a woman who has spontaneous

orgasms. One possible explanation is that sexually arousing fantasies were occurring unconsciously. More common examples that have been well documented recently are the "sleeper effects" in children of divorce. Example: children may be unaware of emotions (fears, anger) during their parents' divorce but suffer ill effects from the divorce years later, often when they become intimate with someone. There are lots of things, especially feelings, going on inside of us that we don't know about. Haven't you felt upset after talking to someone without knowing why? Don't you sometimes respond to events and behaviors very differently than others do, and can't see why you have such a different reaction?

8. You may openly share your feelings with others. This involves many skills: self-disclosure, "I" statements, social skills, assertiveness, self-confidence etc. Telling your story, as in therapy, self-help groups, or with friends, is usually healthy (as long as you share your emotions and don't just stick to the objective facts, and as long as the listeners are supportive).

9. You may use your feelings as a barometer of your relationships with others and your self-acceptance. Negative, unwanted feelings are a sign that something needs to be changed, that self-help is needed.

Now we will look at ways to take control of your emotions.

Understanding your emotions, behavior, feelings, physiology, and thoughts will help you plan ways to change them.

First, don't forget that focusing on the behavior or changing the environment can also reduce an unpleasant emotion, e.g. reduce your fear by putting better locks on the doors or by avoiding someone you are mad at. Fears can also be reduced by modeling someone who is less afraid than you are. You can develop other behaviors that will counteract the unwanted emotions, e.g. activity counteracts depression, assertion counteracts anger, facing the fear counteracts it, relaxation counteracts the hyperactivity of the workaholic, etc. Contrary to the notion that "time heals," there is evidence, that fears, grief, memory of a trauma, etc. don't just fade away. These feeling do decline if we repeatedly expose ourselves to the upsetting situation or memory over and over again while relaxed or under less stressful conditions (yet, becoming very distraught while talking to friends about the "awful" situation doesn't usually help). However, changing the consequences of a behavior can alter emotions also, e.g. ask your friends to praise your healthy assertiveness and challenge your mousy conformity.

Second, don't forget that our thoughts strongly influence our emotions. And, since we can sometimes change our thoughts and since psychology is in a "cognitive" era, there is great emphasis on cognitive methods at this time.

The methods here deal with basic raw emotions: anxiety or fears, anger, and sadness. Of course, these same methods can be used on the emotional part of any other problem. Passive-dependent problems tend to be handled with cognitive-behavioral methods and new skills.

Emotions are a crucial part of our lives and they are fascinating. Several recent books will help you understand. Follow the steps below to learn how to manage and have a control over your emotions;

1. Identify What You're Really Feeling

When you're experiencing this negative emotion or Action Signal, ask yourself, "What am I really feeling right now?" Get clarity on the emotion. "Am I feeling angry, or is it something else?"

2. Understand the message of your emotions- They Serve You

Understanding helps you master your emotion, solve the challenge, and prevent the same problem from occurring in the future. Here's some Empowering Questions to find the empowering meaning in any negative emotion or situation:

a) What else could this mean?

b) What can I learn from this?

c) How do I want to feel?

d) What would I have to believe to feel that way right now?

e) What am I willing to do about it right now?

3. Find Confidence

The fastest, simplest, and most powerful way to handle any emotion is to remember a time when you felt a similar emotion and realize that you've successfully handled this emotion before. If you handled it in the past, you can handle it again today. Ask yourself, "What did I do then to deal with this emotion?" If you do the same things, you will get similar results.

4. Get Certain You Can Handle This Not Only Today, But In The Future As Well

Again, you want to remember the ways you've handled this negative emotion in the past, and rehearse handling situations where this Action Signal would come up in the future. Ask yourself, "What are 3-4 ways I could change my perception when an Action Signal comes up?"

Here's a few suggestions:

To change your perception, ask yourself, "What else could this mean?" or "What's great about this?" Another great question would be, "What can I do now to feel the way I want?" At first your brain might say, "NOTHING!" But if you push yourself and keep asking, you will come up with an answer.

5. Take Action

The final step is to get excited of the fact that you can easily handle this emotion and take some action right away to prove that you've handled it. And when is the best time to handle an emotion? When you first begin to feel it! You want to kill the monster while it's little. Obviously, to know how to master your emotions takes practice. The more that you use these 6 steps to emotional mastery, the better you will get at mastering your emotions.

Every negative emotion has a message or call to action it's trying to give you. We want to identify that message, then learn and use our emotions to better us.

1. Discomfort

This is also known as boredom, impatient, unease, distress, or mild embarrassment.

Message: Discomfort is a GOOD THING because it is your subconscious telling you that you can be more. The message is, you need to either change your perception or change your actions.

Solution: a) Use the Emotional Forces to change your state. b) Clarify what you do want. c) Refine your actions. Try a different approach and see if you can immediately change the way you're feeling about the situation, and/or change the quality of results you're producing.

2. Fear

This is also known as low levels of concern, intense worry, anxiety, fright, and terror.

Message: The anticipation that something that's going to happen soon needs to be prepared for. This is good, as it gives you massive energy to prepare.

Solution: a) Review what you're feeling fearful about and evaluate what you must do to prepare yourself mentally. Figure out what actions you need to take to deal with the situation in the best possible way. b) To antidote your fear, make the decision to have faith. Know that you've done all you can to prepare, and understand that very few fears in life ever come to fruition.

3. Hurt

Also known as a sense of loss or having an expectation not met.

Message: We have expectations that has not been met. Or, there's been a loss of intimacy or trust. This is good, because it shows you have a big heart and care about your life.

Solution: a) Realize that in reality you may not have lost anything. Maybe what you need to lose is the false perception that this person is trying to wound or hurt you. b) Re-evaluate the situation. Is there really loss here? Or am I judging this situation too soon, or too harshly? c) Elegantly and appropriately communicate your feeling of loss to the person involved? For example, "The other day when x-y-z happened, I misinterpreted it to mean that you didn't care, and I have a sense of loss. Can you clarify for me what really happened?"

4. Anger

Also known as resentful, furious, enraged, or irritated.

Message: An important rule or standard that you hold for your life has been violated by someone else, or maybe by you. This is good, as it gives you a passion and fire for you to make things right.

Solution: a) Realize you may have misinterpreted the situation completely. Maybe the person breaking your rules don't realize how important it is to you. b) Realize that even if a person did violate one of your standards, your rules are not necessarily the "right" rules. c) Ask more empowering questions: "In the long run, is it true that this person really cares about me?", "What can I learn from this?", "How can I communicate the importance of these standards I hold myself to this person in a way that causes them to want to help me and not violate my standards again in the future?"

5. Frustration

Message: This is an exciting signal. It means your brain believes you could be doing better than you currently are. The solution is within range, but what you're currently doing isn't working, and you need to change your approach. This signal is telling you to be more flexible in your approach.

Solution: a) Realize frustration is your friend. Brainstorm ways to get a result. How can you flex your approach? b) Get input on how to deal with the situation. Find a role model, someone who has found a way to get what you want. c) Get fascinated by what you can learn that could help you handle this challenge not only today, but in the future.

6. Disappointment

Also known as being let down, sad or defeated.

Message: An expectation you have had is probably not going to happen, so it's time to change your expectations to make them more appropriate for this situation, take action to set and achieve a new goal immediately. This is good as it shows the depth of the caring you have and the high standards your set.

Solution: a) Immediately figure out what you can learn from the situation that could help you achieve teh very thing you're after in the first place. b) Set a new goal, something that will be even more inspiring, and something you can make immediate progress toward. c) Realize you may be judging too soon. Often it's just a temporary challenge. Remember, "God's delays are not

God's denials." You may just be in "lag time", or have unrealistic expectations. d) Realize the situation isn't over yet and develop more patience. Re-evaluate what you want and develop a more effective plan. e) Cultivate an attitude of positive expectancy about what will happen in the future, regardless of what occurred in the past.

7. Guilt

Also known as remorse or regret.

Message: Tells you that you've violated one of your own highest standards and must do something immediately to ensure you're not going to violate that standard again. This is a good, because it's your internal compass for doing what you believe to be right.

Solution: a) Acknowledge that you have violated a critical standard you have for yourself. b) Absolutely commit yourself to make sure this behavior will never happen again in the future. c) Rehearse in your mind how, if you could live it again, you could deal with the same situation you feel guilty about in a way that is consistent with your own highest personal standards. Utilize guilt to drive you to hold yourself to a higher standard in the future.

8. Inadequacy

Also known as unworthiness, anytime we feel we can't do something we should be able to do.

Message: That you don't presently have a level of skill necessary for the task at hand. You need more information, understanding, strategies, tools, or confidence. This is good because it moves you to learn, grow and contribute to others.

Solution: a) Ask yourself, "Is this really an appropriate emotion for me to feel in this situation?" "Am I really inadequate, or do I need to change my perception?" If so, then you need to find a way to do something better than you've done before. b) Appreciate the encouragement to improve. Understand you don't need to be perfect. You can begin to feel adequate by

committing to constant and never-ending improvement.
c) Find a role model – get coaching from them.

9. Overload Or Overwhelm

Also known as grief, depression and helplessness.

Message: Re-evaluate what's most important to you in this situation. May have unrealistic expectations of trying to deal with too many things at once, or trying to change things overnight. Grief happens when you feel like there's no empowering meaning, or your life is being negatively impacted by people, events, or forces that are outside of your control.

Solution: a) Decide what the most important thing to focus on is. b) Write down all the important things and put them in a list of priority. c) Tackle the first thing on your list, continue to take action until mastered it. d) Start focusing on what you can control. Realize there must be an empowering meaning.

10. Loneliness

Also known as feeling alone, apart, or separate.

Message: The Need to connect with people. This is good because it shows your love of people.

Solution: a) Realize you can reach out and make a connection immediately and end the loneliness. There are caring people everywhere. b) Identify what kind of connection you need. c) Remind yourself that what's really great about being lonely means, "I really care about people, and I love to be with them. I need to find out what kind of connection I need with somebody right now, and then take an action immediately to make it happen." d) Reach out and connect.

Chapter Two

How To Turn Negative Feelings Into Positive Attitudes

How many times have you heard a friend, co-worker, spouse or significant other say, "Think positive" when you are feeling depressed, angry, anxious, frustrated or just down-right negative? Usually it's the last think you want to hear at the moment, but it could possibly be the best thing you could do for both your emotional and physical health! Positive attitude, positive thinking, and optimism are now known to be a root cause of many positive life benefits. Studies show positive people can experience an increased life span, lower rates of depression, lower levels of stress, greater resistance to the common cold, better overall well-being, reduced risk of death from cardiovascular disease and better coping skills during times of hardship and stress. It seems people with a positive attitude simply live longer, happier, healthier, more successful lives... and who doesn't want that!!

Attitude is defined as the mental position that represents an individual's degree of like or dislike for an item - a generally positive or negative view of a person, place, thing, or event. A positive attitude is, therefore, the inclination to generally be in an optimistic, hopeful state of mind. However, attitudes are expected to change as a function of experience - so someone with a typically negative attitude can change! Overall, people with a positive attitude are optimists and believe they are accountable for good things and that good things will generally come their way.

If something bad comes instead, optimists tend to write it off as an isolated incident, an anomaly, or something out of their control. They continue to believe things will be better in the future. A pessimist is a person who nurtures a consistently negative attitude, expecting the worst of people and of situations. This outlook can persist regardless of facts or circumstances that might indicate a more balanced or positive reality. It is your attitude, not your aptitude that determines your altitude. Sure you need skills, but you can learn skills - in fact a positive attitude will make it much more likely that you will learn the skills necessary to succeed. If you take two people with an equal skill set the person with the better attitude will win. Unfortunately it is not always easy to stay positive and keep a good attitude. As things go wrong throughout your day, it is easy to let negative thoughts start to take over. Thankfully there are many things that you can do to help maintain a positive attitude.

However, your way of thinking, whether positive or negative, is a habit… and habits can be changed! But it takes practice. If your first thoughts about the meaning of something that has happened are negative thoughts, take the first step toward a positive attitude by simply recognizing your thoughts as negative and trying to create a more positive thought. Thoughts are always under your control and can be changed! The following steps can also help you create a more positive attitude.

It has been estimated that the average person has roughly 60,000 individual thoughts every 24 hours. 95 percent of these thoughts are the same they had the previous day, and 80 percent of these repeated thoughts are of a negative/pessimistic nature. Furthermore, many of these pessimistic thoughts are unconscious and habitual, meaning that people have next to no awareness of the impact that these thoughts have over their lives.

What is even more worrisome is that 95 percent of the thoughts that people have form the foundations of the emotions they experience throughout the day. This is significant because our emotions form the foundations of our attitude, and our attitude is what shapes our happiness and success in all areas of life.

Negativity is the greatest curse that one could ever come out of. Negativity is that demon which rules and kicks all the positive and good qualities of an individual, leading him towards a downfall. A negative mind is reluctant to grow and also it affects the smooth flow of the life.

An attitude is a thought, feeling, or belief, while a behavior is an action that others can see you doing. Attitudes are internal, and behaviors are external. The attitudes and behaviors of a healthy, reasonable person are usually in harmony. Whatever you're feeling, you're creating. If you're worried about money matters and experiencing a sense of want, you create a feeling of lack instead of abundance, and your finances worsen. Alternately, if you create a feeling of abundance instead of want, your financial prospects improve.

A negative attitude carries with it a lack of awareness. You're not necessarily aware of a negative attitude permeating your outlook on life, and because of this lack of awareness, your attitude affects your interactions with other people and your interactions with yourself.

What if you were to become aware? What if, suddenly, you were able to step outside of the thought pattern that creates your attitude, choose a new pattern, and thus, a new attitude? Think about your thoughts. Many sources of advice aren't going to tell you this crucial point: Changing your attitude is not about stifling or eliminating negative thoughts. It's about changing your thought patterns through action.

Negative thoughts will arise, but when you brood on them it's like feeding and rewarding them so that they will come back again and form a pattern. When you alter repetitive thought patterns, you alter your attitude it's a physical process, and with it comes the ability to change the world in which you live. You'll achieve things you didn't think were possible before. To undertake this change, understand what to do with negative or unhelpful thoughts when they arise. This understanding will help you take action towards changing your attitude.

People with a positive attitude make things happen or, as baseball executive Branch Rickey once noted, "Luck is the residue of design." He meant that if you plan things right and have the right attitude, you'll be prepared if things fall into place. It's not really luck at all. You made it happen. Think about it. Do you want to hang around with people who are always saying things like, "I'm no good at anything," "I never get a break," or "I don't feel like doing anything"? That kind of thinking is not only depressing: It's contagious. If you want to be a winner (and who doesn't?), you need to think like a winner. And thinking like a winner starts with taking some concrete steps toward your goal. Let's look at a few things you can do to develop a winning attitude.

Having a positive attitude is important, indeed. It's important not only when it comes to how you view yourself but also when it comes to viewing life in general. Admittedly, thinking in a positive way is not always easy especially as you deal with life's ups and downs. But it is possible! Once you start to recognize the positive things that already exist in your life and learn how to see them even in the face of adversity, positive thinking can become YOUR mode of thinking.

People with positive attitudes believe they have within themselves the ability to overcome many obstacles. No matter what life hands them, their ability to think positively gets them through even the most difficult situations. "Attitudes are more important than facts," according to famed psychiatrist Dr. Karl Menninger. If you have a defeatist attitude, then you believe you're a failure whether you really are one or not.

Thoughts are biochemical impulses of energy, intelligence, and information that hold magnetic properties. These magnetic properties originate within each cell and are influenced by your peer groups, worldviews, cultural history, media, religion, mythology and as a result of social expectations. All of these elements of life influence and shape the thoughts you have about yourself, about others and about your life and circumstances. Over time, these thoughts evolve from opinions into beliefs and convictions.

Beliefs and convictions are nothing more than a recipe for thoughts that have been "locked" into place. When you have a belief about something, there is no doubting or wishing or hoping. Things are the way they are and there is no alternate view. You have "locked" a certain set of thoughts in place to form this belief, and this belief is part of the puzzle that shapes your attitude throughout the day.

Let's break this down another way: Your thoughts are a result of "life". You have the thoughts you have, because of how you've been influenced by "life". Life includes what is now, what was in the past, and what you expect to happen in the future. As such, your thoughts and the attitudes you have are a result of your peer groups, worldviews, your cultural history, media influences, religious traditions and beliefs, and other social factors. In other words, you have the thoughts you have because you've experienced life in a certain and specific way. Therefore, you are how you are today because of the influences you have allowed into your life into your mind.

Over a lifetime you have chosen to focus on certain things while ignoring other things. There are so many different beliefs, opinions, and perspectives in this world. However, you have only chosen to focus on a few of them. Some of them have been somewhat forced upon you by your peers, parents, teachers, mentors, culture and religious background. However, other things you have chosen to focus on because of your personal preferences and tastes. You have therefore created your current thought-patterns and perspectives through the choices you have made over a lifetime.

Thoughts don't immediately turn into beliefs and/or attitudes. It's a process that takes time. You will, for instance, have an initial thought about something. This thought stimulates various cells in your brain. The more you use this "thought" through repetition, the more you use those particular cells, and the stronger the connection between those cells becomes. Likewise, the more emotional intensity that goes into a thought, the more the neural highway in the brain strengthens. As such, the easier it is to have that particular "thought" the next time around. Eventually, the thought becomes a habit and is projected out into the external world as an attitude; which is nothing more than a collection of thoughts, beliefs, opinions, and values.

A thought is never an isolated event. Your brain always tries to make sense of the world by linking present circumstances to past memories. This connection between the past and present forms associations in the brain that help you make better sense of the world. You might, of course, learn something new and different, however, your brain will still attempt to find some relevance, and will, therefore, find a way to connect the new with the old.

How your brain connects the new experiences to the old memories will determine how you make sense of the world. And how you make sense of the world shapes how you think about your world; which builds the foundations of what you believe about your world — manifesting in the attitude you project out into the world.

Thoughts are as complex as they are simple. They are simple because of their nature. It's just easy to have a thought, however, it's not easy to understand how that thought came to be, or what the consequences of having that thought will be in the future. As such, your thoughts are very complex structures because they are influenced by many different factors.

The Fundamentals Of An Attitude

Your attitude is in many ways nothing more than a collection of your values, beliefs and the opinions you have about a specific subject. These parts of your psyche are shaped by your thoughts, and your thoughts are shaped by the world you live in, by your past memories, and as a result of the things you have chosen to focus on over a lifetime.

Whatever you give your attention to becomes a priority in your life. Therefore, whatever you decide to focus on has meaning for you, and as a result, these things will shape how you think, what you believe, what you value, and essentially the attitude you will project out into the world.

There are two Universal Laws at play here. The first of these laws is the Law of Concentration, and the second of these laws is the Law of Becoming.

Law of Concentration: The Law of Concentration states that what you think, emotionalize and visualize continuously grows in your life.

Law of Becoming: The Law of Becoming states that you transform yourself in accordance with your dominant thought patterns. In other words, you attract into your life your weaknesses, strengths, limitations, and abilities in accordance with the thoughts you have chosen to dwell upon most often throughout the day.

These two Universal Laws are basically saying that your entire life and the attitude you project out into the world is dependent upon what you choose to focus on most of the time. Therefore, if your attitude is poor and you desire to make a change, then you must choose to focus on other things that will help you transform your thoughts; thereby improving your state-of-mind (attitude).

Your attitude is also tied to the references that you have collected over a lifetime.

Every experience you have — whether good or bad, painful or pleasurable — creates a set of memories. These memories form references that you use to make sense of the world you live in. These references are just experiences that have come about as a result of pain and pleasure in your life. You might, for instance, have experienced a negative situation in the past which brought you painful memories. Or you might have experienced a positive situation in the past which brought you pleasurable memories. These situations/experiences are nothing more but memories today. However, these memories/references have a significant impact on the attitude you project out into the world.

Your brain will naturally connect many painful memories/references together to form an opinion about something. These opinions strengthen over time as more related references are found. And over the long-term, these references come to form your beliefs about this specific situation or area of your life. And consequently, these beliefs form the foundations of the attitude you project out into the world.

Now, it's important to note that these memories/references are only opinions. They are only your perspectives and interpretations of the situation. They might have no actual basis in reality. As such, your attitude might be based on false references and distorted memories that you have accepted as the truth. Your negative attitude is therefore based on a "lie" that you have convinced yourself to believe. And this is influencing how you feel, think and behave in specific situations for better or worse. What's even worse, is that it influences your expectations of yourself, of others and of the world around you. This, therefore, creates a "snowball" effect where a negative attitude grows and picks up momentum over time until it destroys your life.

One day after years of living with a negative mental attitude, you might experience some very intense pain that results from the attitude you consistently project out into the world. It's this painful experience that will often provide you with the "wake-up" call you need to make some changes for the better. But in all honesty, you don't need to wait until this moment arrives. You can start making positive changes today right now!

Focusing On The Positives

Every individual has a different set of abilities. Where you do well, another person might fail. Likewise, something that comes easily to another person might be difficult for you. No matter what your strengths and weaknesses, it's important to believe in your own abilities. When you focus on areas where you are successful, you will build your self-confidence. And with a strong sense of self-confidence, your chances for success and happiness will be greater.

Think of a situation that has you worried. Write a sentence describing that situation. Then make a list NOT of the factors that are against you but the factors that are for you. It may surprise you how many positive things you really have going for you.

Are you generous with your positive thoughts? Do you share them with others in the form of compliments and praise? You might be surprised to discover that, like most people, you're a little stingy when it comes to sharing a nice thought about someone else. It's one thing to THINK something positive about another person and quite another to actually tell him or her. Sharing kind words and statements with others is an important step in learning to focus on the positives in life. When we learn to see the good in other people, we learn to see the good in ourselves (and vice versa!).

A Positive Mental Attitude (PMA) is the ability to interpret and reframe your life experiences in a favorable way that is helpful and advantageous in relation to the desired outcomes you would like to achieve. It is the ability to cultivate optimism during difficult times. In other words, it's a "solution-focused" attitude that seeks out answers over complaints.

Cultivating a PMA takes time and practice. It's not something you'll immediately get into the habit of doing. You'll need to make some changes, start doing things differently and make some better choices. It's a process that takes some effort, however, it will be effort worth spent as it will help open the door to very different perspectives and a world full of new opportunities.

Let's now take a look at some simple things you can do to help shift how you think about your life and circumstances that will help encourage a PMA.

Empower Your Language

The words you use to express yourself are emotional triggers that significantly influence your state-of-mind and the attitude you bring forth into every situation. These words either create positive expectations, or they create limiting and negative expectations. It all depends on the words you decide to use.

In order to overcome a negative mental attitude you must transform your language, and transforming your language begins by changing the words you habitually use when in a negative state-of-mind. You can do this in one of two ways:

• You can lower the intensity of the negative words you use.

• You can change negative words into positive words.

For instance, you might choose to lower the intensity of the words you use by changing "I am feeling angry…" to "I am feeling concerned…". Or you might instead choose to put a positive spin on things by changing "I am feeling angry…" to "I am kind of curious…".

The second choice is the better option; however, this can also be the most difficult option because it forces you to think in a very different way that might significantly go against your habitual tendencies. This can, therefore, create some internal resistance and conflict. If this resistance is very evident in your situation, then you might instead choose the first option, where you lower the intensity of the negative word you are using. This helps you feel somewhat better about the situation but doesn't necessarily conflict with your habitual thinking patterns.

You might initially begin using the first option, where you consciously lower the intensity of the words you are expressing. Then once you begin feeling more comfortable with these words, you can switch to the second option where you replace your limiting words with more empowering words that can be more helpful in your situation. As such, over time you will begin to shift your attitude from a negative to a more positive state-of-mind. However, all this requires conscious effort, and it may be difficult at first, however, with some persistent effort you can successfully make these changes.

When it comes to the language you choose to use, it's important that you set positive expectations for yourself. For example, is there any point being angry in this situation? By being angry you are drawing into your attention all the things that make you feel angry, and as a result, you feel even angrier, which ends up creating expectations that there will be more things to feel angry about in the future. Maybe instead of feeling angry, you can feel a little concerned or somewhat curious. Both states-of-mind will dramatically shift how you think about the situation, and this will subsequently create a different set of expectations moving forward. Moreover, your attitude will improve and you will be in a far more advantageous position to make the very best of this situation.

There are a lot of possibilities here. All that's required is that you play around with the words you use. Don't settle on one kind of word. Instead, focus on adding richness and color to your language that will help you shift how you think and interpret the events and circumstances of your life.

The words you use and the thoughts you indulge in influence your physiology. Likewise, your physiology influences the words you choose to use and the thoughts you choose to indulge in. Therefore by making small shifts in your physiology can help you to think different thoughts. And when you think different thoughts, you will choose to use different words to express your opinions and feelings. And as your words change, so does your attitude.

This again will not be easy. You probably have certain ways that you tend to habitually use your body when you're in a bad mood. These habits will not be easy to break and will initially require some conscious effort. In fact, you might need to "will" your body to move a certain way, to breathe a certain way, or to stand a certain way in order to break your habitual patterns. However, with persistent effort you will make progress, and this is what will help you to shift to a more positive state-of-mind.

It's human nature to make comparisons. Some people make comparisons to others, while others make comparisons to their "best selves". Both are helpful at certain times. For instance, self-to-other comparisons help you gauge where other people are at, and this helps fuel your competitive spirit. However, it can also make you feel inadequate and incapable if you fail to live up to other people's standards and results. On the other hand, there are self-to-self comparisons. Making these comparisons is helpful because you are competing against your best self.

All this is relevant to attitude because often a poor mental attitude is linked to self-to-self comparisons. We consciously or unconsciously compare ourselves to others in an attempt to make ourselves feel better about ourselves. However, if we are unable to live up to the standards that other people set, then it's easy to feel somewhat worthless and inadequate. And it's from this place that a negative mental attitude often comes to the surface and manifests in excuses and complaints.

To avoid this scenario, choose instead to only make self-to-self comparisons. Compare yourself to your best self, and leave the self-to-other comparisons to others.

Cultivate Present Moment Awareness

The reason why you have a poor mental attitude is because you have all these unfulfilled expectations that are weighing heavily on your shoulders.

When in a negative state of mind you're either indulging in the past by holding onto grudges, regrets, and anger. Or you are focusing on the future filled with fear, anxiety, and uncertainty. Focusing on the past or future brings you no respite or relief. So what's the point of focusing in this way? Instead, encourage yourself to focus on being more mindful of the present moment.

Within the present moment, there are no regrets, there is no anger, and there is no fear or anxiety. All that exists in the present moment is choice and opportunity. In the present moment, you can only focus on what's before you, right here, right now. And what's before you presents you with an opportunity to choose a better path moving forward. However, in order to find that opportunity in the present moment, you must "get out of your head" and let go of all your expectations, hurts, fears, anxieties, etc. You will only change by letting these things go, and the best way to do that is to become mindful of the present moment.

Ask Effective Questions

Whether you are consciously aware of it or not, you are always asking questions. Some questions are helpful, while others may not be so helpful, and will, therefore, tend to prolong a poor mental attitude.

The great thing about questions is that they help direct your focus and attention to specific things. When for instance you are focusing on the negatives and on what's not working, then you will tend to feel miserable, and that will come across in the attitude you project out into the world. However, when you're focusing on what's working, on what you have, and on what you can control, then your attitude likewise changes. You are no longer feeling regret, disappointment, or complaining about things. You are instead focused on the things that can help you move forward in a more positive way.

Questions will help you direct your "focus" in exactly this way. However, you will, of course, need to ask yourself the right kinds of questions to help focus your mind on the things that will help encourage a positive mental attitude.

There is a reason why you might have a poor attitude. And that often comes down to the company you keep. The attitude you consistently project into the world probably very closely resembles the attitude of your peers. Therefore, if their attitude is poor, then your attitude will also be poor. If they always complain, make excuses, blame and focus on problems, then you probably also do this. This, of course, will not be true in all cases. However, for the most part, your five closest peers/friends will often mirror your attitude as much as you mirror their attitude. For this very reason, it's absolutely critical that you select the people you choose to hang out with very carefully.

Getting Rid Of The Negatives

It is natural for people to develop negative thoughts and feelings. Although it is not easy to get rid of these "negatives," it's important that people learn to focus instead on more positive thoughts and ideas. What if individuals focus more on how to get rid of negative attitudes and practice the skills necessary to replace negative thoughts and feelings and cultivate a more positive attitude?

Like everyone else, you have negative thoughts and feelings fear, insecurity, guilt, and even hatred. But also, like everyone else, you have within yourself the ability to replace these "negatives" with a more positive way of thinking. It may not always be easy, but it is possible!

Are you a user of "little negatives"? Do such phrases as "I don't think I can do that" or "I'm afraid I'll be late" clutter up your conversation? You may not even realize it when you use negatives words and phrases. Regardless, if you use them enough, they can condition you to think negatively, too. Before you know it, little negatives will clutter up your mind, as well as your conversation.

Everyone is guilty of using little negatives once in a while.

Often, it's not the "little negatives" that stand in the way of a positive attitude. It's the big ones! People who consistently talk negatively not only affect themselves and their attitudes but others who are around them. On the other hand, people who carry on personal and group conversations with upbeat words and expressions give themselves and others plenty to be positive about.

When people feel inferior, they are easily discouraged and can even become depressed. Instead of focusing on the things they can do well, they dwell on their weaknesses and failures. What causes feelings of inferiority? Many times, these feelings begin in childhood. A person might think he or she is too fat, or too thin, or not like other children. Often, feelings of inferiority come from fears the fear of making new friends or the fear of failure, for example. (One poll found that the No. 1 fear is speaking in public. It even ranked above death!)

Everyone has fears. Finding ways to deal with those fears is an important step in conquering them. See for yourself.

Have you ever noticed the tempo of things around you? If you listen to the wind in the trees or the buzzing of insects, you'll notice that nature has a very even pace. But if you listen to the traffic on city streets or the sounds of people shopping during the holiday rush, you'll realize that most of us speed around at an unnatural pace. The problem with this frantic pace of living is that too often people don't take enough time to rest and relax. Even young people need to take time to give their minds and bodies a break. It can restore your energy, ease the stress and tension in your life, and, yes, help you maintain a positive outlook.

An effective technique for restoring your mind's "energy" is the daily practice of silence. Many experts recommend taking 10 to 15 minutes out of every day to spend in the quietest place available. Do not read, write, or listen to music. Just practice throwing your mind into neutral and saturating your thoughts with peaceful experiences, words, and ideas.

Knute Rockne, one of the greatest football coaches in history, said, "I have to get the most energy out of a man, and I have discovered that it cannot be done if he hates another man. Hate blocks his energy, and he isn't up to par until he eliminates it and develops a friendly feeling." Hate is just one example of our so-called energy blockers. Fear and resentment can also zap away our energy mentally and physically. If we can keep our minds free of the bad feelings and inner conflicts that we allow to affect us, our bodies can operate like a finely tuned machine, full of energy and raring to go.

A famous politician once traveled hundreds of miles, making seven speeches in one day. Someone asked him how he could still be so full of energy after such a long day. He replied, "Because I believe absolutely in everything I said in those speeches. I am enthusiastic about my convictions." When you truly believe in something, you often find you have unlimited energy. Perhaps it's a certain cause or charity. Maybe it's a special group or community organization. Whatever your good cause, finding a way to keep your mind interested and active is one way to keep the energy flowing and your attitude positive.

Finding Happiness

Happiness often depends on how you view life's situations. Some people dwell on what's wrong in their lives; others concentrate on the good things life gives them.

This lesson is designed to help individuals focus on sources of happiness already in place in their lives and to increase their happiness and maintain a positive approach to life. Humans are guided through activities that develop attitudes and actions that promote individual happiness.

Who decides if you're going to be happy or unhappy? You do! Abraham Lincoln once said that people are as happy as they make up their minds to be. The same message is echoed in the more modern saying, "When life gives you lemons, make lemonade." It's true that we can't control everything that happens to us. However, we can adjust our attitudes to avoid feeling overwhelmed by life's ups and downs. Some of the things that worry us in our daily lives can be traced to the society in which we live. We may not be able to control crime in our cities, the rising unemployment rate in our state, or the prejudiced attitudes of others. But our thoughts and attitudes can help us overcome the negative feelings that result from such worries.

With practice, you can drive off the thoughts that make you unhappy. Dr. Norman Vincent Peale, famous for his newspaper columns and self-help books on positive thinking, suggests starting each morning saying something positive to yourself, such as:

"I believe I can successfully handle all the problems that will arise today. I feel good physically, mentally,

and emotionally. It is wonderful to be alive. I am grateful for all that I have had, for all that I now have,

and for all that I shall have. Things aren't going to fall apart."

There are a few basic principles of happy living, such as a showing kindness to others, having a friendly attitude, sympathizing with someone's sorrow, and showing sensitivity to others' feelings. If you base your actions and attitudes on such fundamental principles, your chances for happiness will greatly increase.

Here are some other basic principles of happy living:

• Keep your heart free from hate

• Keep your mind free from worry

• Live simply

• Give much

• Forget thinking of yourself and think of others

• Treat others as you would like to be treated

Along with developing attitudes and actions to make you a happier person, other factors can contribute to your happiness. For instance, having good friends or having someone to feel close to are "special gifts" that can give you a happier outlook. Another important factor that can lead to happiness is being able to distinguish between your needs and wants. We NEED food, shelter, and other basics for survival. We WANT nice homes and cars, designer clothes, the best stereo system, and more. And those who get carried away thinking these wants will bring them happiness often end up disappointed. After all, "Money can't buy happiness," as the old saying goes.

Expecting The Best

It is important to recognize the mindset of a winner. Local heroes, sports figures, and political leaders all know what it takes to win. In this lesson, we will examine the power of the mind in achieving success. Individuals will become familiar with overcoming obstacles and aiming for success.

Many of our favorite fairy tales tell a story of how "wishing can make it so." In real life, however, wishes usually aren't that powerful. Yet it is true that you will do your best when you decide to put your mind to the task. William James, the famous psychologist, said: "Your belief at the beginning of a doubtful undertaking is the one thing that ensures the successful outcome of your venture." In other words, believing you'll succeed can go a long way in making it happen.

Believe it or not, you can change the way you think. If you're a negative thinker one who expects to fail you can change your thinking style by putting images of positive results in your mind. It's not always easy to do. But with a little practice, you can become a pro at expecting the best and getting it!

Throughout the centuries, people have discovered that when you bring all your energy and power to focus upon attaining the best, it will bring the best to you. Being a positive thinker means turning your thoughts toward the best. Positive thinkers make the news every day. They do something no one else has ever done, or they do something better than anyone has ever done it. Their stories prove over and over again that expecting the best and getting it go hand in hand.

Negative feelings don't just interfere with our happiness and our relationships. They can also interfere with our health. In this lesson, we will recognize the effects negative feelings especially anger have on the body. We will examine alternative responses to emotional situations and will learn to achieve more desirable outcomes.

Ever feel like your stomach is "tied in knots"? Has your head ever felt like it was going to "explode"? Such feelings though physical in nature may often be the result of an emotional experience. In fact, one-third of all illnesses are caused by emotional turmoil of some sort. When you are in the grip of anger, fear, resentment, and other negative feelings, your body feels the real effects. That's why it's so important to recognize these effects and to take steps not to let them control you mentally or physically.

Can anger contribute to a person's ill health? Many scientists say "yes." Research also shows that anger and other feelings such as resentment, hate, grudges, ill will, jealousy, guilt, anger, and irritation are all attitudes that, when they linger, can lead to poor health. Research also shows that a person's attitude can affect the speed at which a person recuperates from illness. It doesn't matter whether a person's negative emotions are experienced slowly over a period of time or whether they are expressed violently all at once. Either way, anger and other negative thoughts can cause the general condition of the body to deteriorate into an unhealthy state.

Anger can be one of the most mentally wrenching, physically draining emotions of all. Sure, there are times when everyone gets angry. But people who are quick to anger or who harbor angry feelings may experience some very unhealthy effects. Just look at some of the things that happen to a person's body when he or she gets angry:

• Fists tend to clench

• The voice rises in pitch

• Muscles tense

• The body becomes rigid

• Adrenaline shoots through the body

It's not a pretty sight!

You've probably heard it said, "Never go to bed angry." That's because the sooner you can resolve your angry feelings, the better able you'll be to put them behind you. Sure, letting go of your anger especially when someone has really hurt your feelings isn't easy. Some people carry their anger around with them for years, causing themselves and others untold physical and emotional problems. But with a little effort, it is possible to "forgive and forget," as another saying goes.

Feeling accepted is an important aspect of adolescence. A large part of a student's self-esteem hinges on his perception that others like him. This unit focuses on developing those positive qualities that make a person like himself and, in turn, make others like him. Every individual has the power to enhance his positive qualities as well as eliminate his negative ones. To be successful in a career, and, ultimately, in life, people need to feel good about themselves.

Everyone wants people to like them and wants to be accepted for who they are. Trouble is, that's not always easy to accomplish. In fact, you'll never get EVERYONE to like you. Some people just don't hit it off. But even the most difficult people and people who are shy and unsociable can win friends and feel accepted especially if they like themselves. A feeling of self-confidence and a healthy self-esteem go a long way in the quest for acceptance in today's world.

While there are no universal traits that guarantee you'll win friends, there are some basic characteristics that will make it easier to feel accepted. Three of those characteristics are:

1. Be confident in your own abilities (In other words: Like yourself!)

2. Be a comfortable, easygoing, pleasant person

3. Have a sincere interest in people

By the same token, there are no universal traits that force people to dislike you. But you can bet that if you are rigid, self-centered, egotistical, and irritable, you will not have an easy time when it comes to making friends. These attitudes work to create natural barriers against building friendships.

People will begin to revise their views of you if you take time to talk with them and show an interest in their lives. Here's one way to do that. At night, before going to bed, picture in your mind each person you have met during the day. As each face comes to mind, think one kind thought about him or her. The more positive things you look for in the people you know, the more positive things you'll find!

It can be a challenge to find admirable or likable qualities in some people. But that shouldn't stop you from trying. The qualities that make people likable are often the same qualities that employers are looking for when they hire someone for a job. Strong character traits, such as a good self-image, and, of course, being a positive thinker, all make a difference when it comes time to get a job.

At some point, you'll find yourself dealing with people of questionable character. It's best to distance yourself from such people and be careful about including them among your friends. Never do something that you know is wrong just because others are doing it. You always have the option of saying "No," and of going to a family member, teacher, counselor, clergy member, or neighbor and talking to him or her in confidence about how you're feeling. Relationships with other people are often complicated. By following the suggestions in this lesson for getting along with and respecting others and yourself, you'll find that developing a positive attitude isn't as hard as you might have thought. And any work it does require will be worthwhile the benefits are lifelong and enormous.

You can also follow below tips to have a change of attitude from negative to positive. The following mentioned are few points that help in bringing change in attitude:

1. First identify the change you want in yourself:

Before reaching out to any solution, there requires some indepth research of the issue. The issue needs to be researched on so that the apt solution could be found easily. So, if you feel that you have the negative attitude, then first thing required to do is identify the change that you want. Know the problem you need to address. When you are done with knowing the issue, the first step towards being positive is achieved.

2. Look out the solution for the problem detected:

The negative people only look for running away from the problems instead of finding out the solutions. So, if you are done by identifying the problem, then reach to another step that is finding the valid solution to solve the problem. Instead of saying no to everything, just say yes, that you can do it and reach out to the web of problems around yourself.

3. Look for some role model:

Everyone should have some role model. Having a role model acts as a motivating factor for an individual. Negativity only rules the lie of individuals who has no motivating factor in life. If you have some spirit to move ahead of someone, or if you have someone in mind like whom you wish to become then it is a step towards achieving positive attitude.

4. Try not to say no:

Every negative person search for things which requires the negative answer, so as to run from doing the task. Saying no to everything is also a sign of showing how much a person is negative. So, if you want to turn your attitude from negative to positive, start saying yes to even those things which you cannot do. This can be the very first step of being positive. So, start saying yes to everything you can do.

5. Try to apply the solution in your daily life:

Whatever solution you find for the problem, try to apply it in your daily life. Using the solution in your daily life will help a negative person live a positive life. Negativity only enters one's life when there is no hope left, or when there is no solution to the problem. So, if you want to build a positive attitude, then try and apply the solutions you find in your daily life and you will be able to become positive.

6. Reach out to maximum people:

Talk to more and more people. When you reach out to maximum people for views and finding solutions to the problems, you will get to know the different thinking. The thinking of the individual affects a lot whether negatively or positively. If you think about solutions means you are positive in your life, but if you think about negative things then you are a negative person. So, talking to maximum people can also help you in being positive as it gives more ideas and solutions to the problems.

7. Stop thinking about the past:

No matter how bad your past has been, just do not think of the past. The past also leads to thinking of negativity. The worst past will lead the person to think negative, even in the future, which only leads to the downfall of an individual. So, stop thinking about the past and look in a positive manner towards the future. This way also, one can turn his or her negative attitude towards the positive one.

8. Think about the change in your life:

The change of attitude brings lot of change in life also. A good attitude will bring a good change while bad attitude will bring a bad change in your life. So, whatever you do, make sure that you think of the near future. How will your future be affected and what change will it bring into the life. So, by this way also one can bring in positive attitude and shed away the negative attitude from the life.

9. Do not have expectations:

One way to lead a happy and positive life is having no expectations from anyone. When we expect from people, the people ought to change. So, that change in promises bring utmost dissatisfaction in life which ultimately brings negativity in life. So, if you want to be happy and lead a positive life, then stop keeping expectations from people.

10. Do not move out to the ones who lead you down:

If you talk to many people, means you might come across many negative one's also. So, when you find any individual who is negative and is not helping you taking away the mess from your life, then move away from that individual. Make sure you do not reach out to those who lead you to the deep-down level. The negativity from the people around should never be welcomed.

11. See positivity in everything:

In every situation there is always some positive thing. Even in the worst situation there is always some good things hidden within. So, it is your duty to search for the positive things in life if you need to shed away the negative attitude from your life.

12. Read good books in life:

In life, one should read as many good books as one can. Books prove to be one of your best partners at times. Reading helps in increasing knowledge though, but it also helps in being positive. What can't be taught by people, is taught by the books indeed. So, if you are not an avid reader, then you should become now because becoming a reader takes you in altogether different world where you will only get happiness and you will be away from the negative things. The books help you to forget the worst you have gone in your life.

13. Count the blessings in life:

A day may be bad but the whole life is never bad. So, start counting the good things happened in your life. Count the happiness you still have. Some people do not even possess what you have. So, in order to be happy in life, first be positive because positivity is not only good for the health but also good for attaining success in life. So, if you want to change your bad attitude into positive one, start counting the happiness that still exist in your life. Only such an attitude will help you achieve your goal.

14. Let go of the negative things:

Do not overthink on anything. Just let go of the things which make you feel bad. The bad things in life only brings sadness. So, just let go of the negative things in life and accept what comes your way. When you let go and do not overthink about everything that comes your way, it means you are heading towards a free-spirited life and more of positivity. This helps you have a positive attitude.

15. Make a list of things you are grateful for:

Even in the life of a poor man, there are days for which he or she is grateful and if it is about you, then you might have more things to be grateful at. So, make a list of the things of which you are really grateful for. Listing all the things you are thankful will help you in counteracting with the negative thoughts that might arise in your life.

16. Make use of the positive words:

Whenever you speak, make sure you utter positive things. For that first of all, you need to think positive, what we think is what we speak and what we speak is what is done. So, in order to speak positive things, first think positive, only then you will be able to use positive words and ultimately the actions would be the same. So, this way also you can improve your attitude by turning from negative to positive.

17. Help others:

When you do some good deed, you feel happy from within. There comes a sense of satisfaction in life. So, help as many people as you can. If not help, do whatever you can do to make people happy. More you extend the possible help; more you grow from zero to next level. So, try and help others as much as you can. Help can be of any type, be it volunteering in a hospital, or any NGO. Doing this, you will be able to choose positivity in your life. Not just this, helping your friends and family can also provide you required happiness in life. Giving and receiving love is all required to live a happy and positive life.

18. Indulge yourself in some work:

So do not sit idle any time. Sitting idle will only lead to negative thoughts. When you are busy with some productive things in life, you ultimately get over all the negative thoughts in life. So, keep yourself as busy as you can and let the negative thoughts get a way to pass away from your life.

19. Meditate a lot:

Meditation and yoga are a way by which you can focus yourself towards positivity. Yoga helps one to stay positive and happy always. It is very relaxing and helps in easing the mind, thus shedding away all the negativity from the life. So, exercise, meditate and do as much yoga as you can.

20. Take an initiative always:

When you start taking the responsibility, you learn to take an initiative of your own. Do not ever play a victim in life, just create your own experiences and create your own life. This will not only lead you have success in life but also it will help in being at the top of the list everytime. Not just this, it also keeps you out of the rush and keeps you on the top everytime. Becoming a leader and not a follower is appreciated by all.

21. No one is perfect, so just move on:

No one is ever perfect and it is said to just move on in life even if you are going through the storms. The storms are the one's which act as a motivating factor for the negative people in life. So, if you want to be positive in life, just stop overthinking on the silly things and give away with the useless things in life. Everyone make mistakes in life but the one who learns from his or her mistake is the one who can succeed. So, even if you make a mistake, make sure you find positivity from that too. Stay happy always and let go of the things which are not important to you. Let the life flow in a smooth manner.

22. Read positive quotes:

Reading positive quotes also help in turning the negative attitude into positive one. The quotes are helpful in time of need and if you do not find people to help you get out of the difficult situations in life, just reach out to the good quotes and inspiring books in your life.

So, above are some of the points on positive and negative attitude and how to improve attitude by turning your negative attitude into positive one. No matter what difficulties you have to counter in life, make sure you stay strong, positive and happy always. Only positive thoughts in the mind can help you gain all what you need in life. Happiness, success and satisfaction in life, all can be achieved when your mind is at peace and mind can only be at peace if you let positivity rule your life.

Positive emotions work collectively like the instruments in a symphony. They harmonize with each other and create the music of life. Nurture any one of them and you'll connect to the endless store of creativity in the universe, raising the volume on other positive feelings as well. It's as if the other emotional instruments can't wait to jump in and create music once you've begun playing even the simplest melody.

You can achieve your destiny by using your creativity and your positive emotions, because feeling any one such emotion will attract events, people, circumstances, and outcomes that resonate to its vibration. Be enthusiastic and enthusiastic people will show up in your life. Experience joy and joyous events will unfold.

Although there are clearly many different types of emotions, they all have some common characteristics. First, emotions are largely non-purposeful and instinctive. The basic emotions that human's express are shared with most mammals. Anyone who has a pet is aware that it's not too difficult to tell when the pet is experiencing emotions like anger, anxiety, and happiness. Second, on the physiological level, as you might expect, emotional behaviors are closely tied to subcortical structures and the autonomic nervous system. This shouldn't be surprising to you in that one of the basic characteristics of the autonomic nervous system is the control of nonpurposeful behaviors such as heart rate and respiration. A third basic characteristic of emotions is that, to a large degree, they appear to be innate. For example, sociologists have found that facial expressions associated with the basic emotions such as fear, anger, and happiness are the same across cultures.

Even with cultures that have had very little contact with the "outside world".

While understanding that negative emotions are a healthy part of life is important, there is a downside to giving them too much free reign.

If you spend too much time dwelling on negative emotions and the situations that might have caused them, you could go into a spiral of rumination. Rumination is the tendency to keep thinking, replaying, or obsessing over negative emotional situations and experiences. In this spiral of negative thinking, you can end up feeling worse and worse about the situation and yourself, the result of which could be a number of detrimental effects to your mental and physical wellbeing.

Another piece of indirect evidence for the innate nature of emotions is illustrated by a muscle located above the eyes called Duchenne's muscle. In the last century it was proposed that one could tell if another person's smile was sincere based on whether or not this muscle contracts. If it does, the smile is sincere, and if it doesn't the smile is not, and, further, this cannot be controlled consciously. Research since this time has supported the existence of this "emotional lie detector" we all carry around like a light bulb on our forehead.

Our focus in this module will be on fear and anxiety. It is not that more positive emotions, like happiness, are not just as important. It is simply that these other emotions have not been studied in depth. Further, the behavioral characteristics of emotions such as happiness and love are more difficult to define empirically than are fear and aggression.

Emotions are an interesting subject; no matter how much somebody denies their existence in their own body, they are still rumbling in the background, affecting your impulses, desires, moods, and humour. In a literal sense, the chemicals in our bloodstream that stimulate our neurons are same chemicals related to your emotions, so you necessarily have emotions at any time. Technically speaking, your mood, even neutral, is an emotion. If a person has low dopamine or serotonin levels, they will likely be experiencing depression. It's an empirical fact.

Consequently, your emotions are intimately tied to your actions; we do things that we enjoy, not necessarily what is easy. People who are addicted to heroin might find themselves running around, figuring out how to get their next hit. This is not an easy course of action, but it leads to a huge reward (a high). Figuring out how to harness your emotions will be a useful tool for your success. If you feel strongly about your success, then you're more likely to take the required actions.

Let's talk about it.

Emotions are not a concrete 'thing'; they are simply a body sensation. Can you feel them? Your body feels certain sensations when you are sad, when you are happy, when you are angry, when you're disgusted, even when you agree or disagree.

If you disagree with this sentiment, try to tune in with your feeling of disagreement. My thoughts on emotions is to learn how to integrate emotions as much as possible to be an integrated human being.

A proposition: What is intrinsically wrong about being okay with feeling what you're feeling in the moment? You don't HAVE to worry about other people's opinion of it, as long as you can handle their opinions (all they can really do is bring up emotions in you).

It's because we fear the consequences that will come from other peoples' reactions. Even when you are alone, what about feeling the emotions in your body and allowing yourself to be present to the sensations? Allowing yourself to sit in the emotions in your body will lead to full-body presence, charisma, etc.. Holding emotions in your body is a useful tool that allows you to become relatable to other people, who become a bit unsettled when they begin to suspect that they're talking to an emotionless robot.

Basic Set Of Emotions

How many emotions are there? In what ways do they vary? There are dozens of emotions. They include anger, contempt, enthusiasm, envy, fear, frustration, disappointment, embarrassment, disgust, happiness, hate, hope, jealousy, joy, love, pride, surprise, and sadness. There have been numerous research efforts to limit and define the dozens of emotions into a fundamental or basic set of emotions. But some researchers argue that it makes no sense to think of basic emotions because even emotions we rarely experience, such as shock, can have a powerful effect on us. Other researchers, even philosophers, argue that there are universal emotions common to all of us. René Descartes, often called the founder of modern philosophy, identified six "simple and primitive passions" wonder, love, hatred, desire, joy, and sadness and argued that "all the others are composed of some of these six or are species of them." Other philosophers (Hume, Hobbes, Spinoza) identified categories of emotions. Though these philosophers were helpful, the burden to provide conclusive evidence for the existence of a basic set of emotions still rests with contemporary researchers. In contemporary research, psychologists have tried to identify basic emotions by studying facial expressions. One problem with this approach is that some motions are too complex to be easily represented on our faces. Take love, for example. Many think of love as the most universal of all emotions, yet it's not easy to express a loving emotion with one's face only. Also, cultures have norms that govern emotional expression, so how we experience an emotion isn't always the same as how we show it. And many companies today offer anger-management programs to teach people to contain or even hide their inner feelings. It's unlikely psychologists or philosophers will ever completely agree on a set of basic emotions, or even whether it makes sense to think of basic emotions. Still, enough researchers have agreed on six essentially universal emotions anger, fear, sadness, happiness, disgust, and surprise with most other emotions subsumed under one of these six categories. Some researchers even plot these six emotions along a continuum: happiness, surprise, fear, sadness, anger, disgust. The closer any two emotions are to each other on this continuum, the more likely it is that people will confuse them. For instance, we some-times mistake happiness for surprise, but rarely do we confuse happiness and disgust. In addition, as we'll see later on, cultural factors can also influence interpretations.

There are some other fundamental aspects of emotions that we need to consider. These aspects include the biology of emotions, the intensity of emotions, their frequency and duration, the relationship between rationality and emotions, and the functions of emotions. Let's deal with each of these aspects in turn.

The Biology of Emotions

All emotions originate in the brain's limbic system, which is about the size of a walnut and near our brain stem. People tend to be happiest (report more positive than negative emotions) when their limbic system is relatively inactive. When the limbic system "heats up," negative emotions such as anger and guilt dominate over positive ones such as joy and happiness. Overall, the limbic system provides a lens through which you interpret events. When it's active, you see things in a negative light. When it's inactive, you interpret information more positively. Not everyone's limbic system is the same. Moderately depressed people have more active limbic systems, particularly when they encounter negative information. And women tend to have more active limbic systems than men, which,

Self-Awareness

Self-awareness is the first component of emotional intelligence which makes sense when one considers that the Delphic oracle gave the advice to "know thyself" thousands of years ago. Self-awareness means having a deep understanding of one's emotions, strengths, weaknesses, needs, and drives. People with strong self-awareness are neither overly critical nor unrealistically hopeful. Rather, they are honest with themselves and with others. People who have a high degree of self-awareness recognize how their feelings affect them, other people, and their job performance. Thus, a self-aware person who knows that tight deadlines bring out the worst in him plans his time carefully and gets his work done well in advance. Another person with high self- awareness will be able to work with a demanding client. She will understand the client's impact on her moods and the deeper reasons for her frustration.

"Their trivial demands take us away from the real work that needs to be done," she might explain. And she will go one step further and turn her anger into something constructive. Self-awareness extends to a person's understanding of his or her values and goals. Someone who is highly self-aware knows where he is headed and why; so, for example, he will be able to be fi rm in turning down a job offer that is tempting financially but does not fi t with his principles or long-term goals. A person who lacks self-awareness is apt to make decisions that bring on inner turmoil by treading on buried values. "The money looked good so I signed on," someone might say two years into a job, "but the work means so little to me that I'm constantly bored." The decisions of self-aware people mesh with their values; consequently, they often find work to be energizing.

How can one recognize self-awareness? First and foremost, it shows itself as candor and an ability to assess oneself realistically. People with high self-awareness are able to speak accurately and openly although not necessarily effusively or concessionally about their emotions and the impact they have on their work. For instance, one manager I know of was skeptical about a new personal-shopper service that her company, a major department-store chain, was about to introduce. Without prompting from her team or her boss, she offered them an explanation: "It's hard for me to get behind the rollout of this service," she admitted, "because I really wanted to run the project, but I wasn't selected. Bear with me while I deal with that." The manager did indeed examine her feelings; a week later, she was supporting the project fully.

Such self-knowledge often shows itself in the hiring process. Ask a candidate to describe a time he got carried away by his feelings and did something he later regretted. Self-aware candidates will be frank in admitting to failure and will often tell their tales with a smile. One of the hallmarks of self-awareness is a self-deprecating sense of humor. Self-awareness can also be identified during performance reviews. Self-aware people know and are comfortable talking about their limitations and strengths, and they often demonstrate a thirst for constructive criticism. By contrast, people with low self-awareness interpret the message that they need to improve as a threat or a sign of failure. Self-aware people can also be recognized by their self-confidence. They have a fi rm grasp of their capabilities and are less likely to set themselves up to fail by, for example, overstretching on assignments. They know, too, when to ask for help. And the risks they take on the job are calculated. They won't ask for a challenge that they know they can't handle alone. They'll play to their strengths. Consider the actions of a midlevel employee who was invited to sit in on a strategy meeting with her company's top executives. Although she was the most junior person in the room, she did not sit there quietly, listening in awestruck or fearful silence.

She knew she had a head for clear logic and the skill to present ideas persuasively, and she offered cogent suggestions about the company's strategy. At the same time, her self-awareness stopped her from wandering into territory where she knew she was weak. Despite the value of having self-aware people in the workplace, my research indicates that senior executives don't often give self-awareness the credit it deserves when they look for potential leaders. Many executives mistake candor about feelings for "wimpiness" and fail to give due respect to employees who openly acknowledge their shortcomings.

Major Emotions

We develop a number of emotions while dealing with different persons and objects in the environment. They can be negative emotions like fear and anxiety or positive emotions like pleasure and love. Let us study these emotions in some detail.

Fear:

Fear is caused by situations which are perceived as physically threatening. The situations that produce fear change with age. During early childhood we are afraid of strange objects and persons, loss of support, darkness and devils etc. During adolescence fears are mostly social in nature (e.g. fear of authority, parental criticism, peer rejection, fear of failure). Maturation and personal experiences contribute to the development of fear. Children learn emotional reactions by imitating their parents, and other family members. That is why a one or two year old child would have no fear of snakes, whereas older children feel quite afraid. Fear can also be developed through conditioning. That is why each person's fear will be somewhat different from that of others. For example, if during childhood somebody was lost in crowd, he or she may develop a fear of crowd. You must have noticed other similar types of fear among your friends such as fear of lizards, darkness etc. When such fears become very strong, they are called phobias. They are unfounded fears. Usually people try to escape fearful situations by running away from them.

Fear is often cited as one of the core basic emotions, and that's because it's heavily linked with our sense of self-preservation. It's an evolved response to warn us about dangerous situations, unexpected obstacles or failures. We don't feel fear in order to feel distressed, on the contrary, it's there to help us navigate potential danger successfully. Embracing the emotion of fear and exploring why it arises can help you prepare yourself proactively to tackle challenges.

Much like fear, anxiety seeks to warn us about potential threats and dangers. It's often seen as a negative emotion as it's thought having an anxious disposition impairs judgment and our ability to act.

Anxiety is a state of painful discomfort of mind. During anxiety a vague fear or apprehension occurs. You may feel anxious if you don't know the exact cause. The difference between fear and anxiety often refers to the involvement of present situation. You can recognize the cause of fear in your present circumstances whereas anxiety may arise due to an anticipated or imaginary situation. You will become anxious when you anticipate any harmful or threatening event. The sense of anxiety can be an unconscious memory of fear arousing stimulus. We may forget the particular unpleasant situation in which we learned a fear. When we face similar situation, we feel anxious without knowing why do we feel so. High level of anxiety is destructive for our performance and health. In extreme cases anxiety may take the form of a mental disorder.

Pleasure:

Pleasure or happiness is a positive emotion which gives satisfaction to the person who experiences it. Pleasure is the reaction to the satisfaction of a need or attainment of a goal. When we are happy, we smile and laugh and there is a clear expression of satisfaction on our faces. An infant express pleasure by babbling. They learn to express happiness in socially approved ways. People derive pleasure from different sources during different stages of life. The babies derive pleasure from physical wellbeing, tickling etc. whereas adults experience pleasure by the experiences like being successful in different situations. Children whose home, school, and neighborhood environments are pleasant have more happy experiences than those who must live, work and play in unpleasant environments.

It is a pleasant emotional reaction directed towards a person, an animal or an object. It is built up as a result of pleasant experience. The most primitive basis of affection is associated with warmth of mother's body, and being fondled and cuddled. Learning plays an important role in determining the persons or objects to which child's affection becomes attached. Children indiscriminately show affection towards members of the family, pets and toys. As adolescence approaches, affection is diverted more towards people than pets. Affectionate responses are shown in an outgoing striving and approach behaviors. Affection is expressed by patting, hugging, verbal expression, protecting and helping the loved one.

Sadness:

When you miss a deadline, get a bad grade, or don't secure that job you had your hopes pinned on, you'll probably feel sad. Sadness happens when we are dissatisfied with ourselves, our achievements or the behavior of someone else around us. Sadness can be good to experience as it indicates to us that we passionate about something. It can be a great catalyst to pursue change.

Guilt is a complex emotion. We can feel this in relation to ourselves and past behaviors that we wish hadn't happened, but also in relation to how our behavior impacts those around us. Guilt is often referred to as a 'moral emotion' and can be another strong catalyst to encourage us to make changes in our life.

Like guilt, apathy can be a complex emotion. If you've lost enthusiasm, motivation or interest in the things you've previously enjoyed, this could be related to apathy. Like anger, it can arise when we lose control over a scenario or situation but instead of becoming angry, we pursue a more passive-aggressive expression of rebellion.

Despair: Ever tried to achieve a certain task or goal multiple times and not succeeded? Did that make you feel like throwing your hands in the air, and camping out in bed with a large tub of ice cream for company? That's despair and it's an emotion that arises when we aren't getting the results we want. Despair gives us an excuse to give up on our desired goals and it comes back to a self-preservation tactic. Despair can actually be a useful reminder to take a break and restore, before continuing to pursue a challenging goal.

Chapter Four
Stress Management

Stress is inevitable and often seems uncontrollable, but we do have the power to control how we let stress affect us. Learning the different tips on how to reduce stress will help you eliminate the stress you are faced with on a daily basis.

As you might imagine, stress affects emotions and moods. For example, students have higher levels of fear before an exam, but their fear dissipates once the exam is over.43 At work, stressful daily events (a nasty email, an impending deadline, the loss of a big sale, being reprimanded by your boss, and so on) negatively affect employees' moods. Also, the effects of stress build over time. As the authors of one study note, "a constant diet of even low-level stressful events has the potential to cause workers to experience gradually increasing levels of strain over time."44 Such mounting levels of stress and strain at work can worsen our moods, and we experience more negative emotions. Consider the following entry from a worker's blog: "i'm in a bit of a blah mood today . . . physically, i feel funky, though and the weather out combined with the amount of personal and work i need to get done are getting to me." Although sometimes we thrive on stress, for most of us, like this blogger, stress begins to take its toll on our mood.

It may seem that there's nothing you can do about your stress level. The bills aren't going to stop coming, there will never be more hours in the day for all your errands, and your career or family responsibilities will always be demanding. But you have a lot more control than you might think. In fact, the simple realization that you're in control of your life is the foundation of stress management.

Managing stress is all about taking charge: taking charge of your thoughts, your emotions, your schedule, your environment and the way you deal with problems.

The ultimate goal is a balanced life, with time for work, relationships, relaxation and fun - plus the resilience to hold up under pressure and meet challenges head on.

Stress management starts with identifying the sources of stress in your life. This isn't as easy as it sounds. Your true sources of stress aren't always obvious and it's all too easy to overlook your own stress-inducing thoughts, feelings, and behaviours. Sure, you may know that you're constantly worried about work deadlines. But maybe it's your procrastination, rather than the actual job demands, that leads to deadline stress.

To identify your true sources of stress, look closely at your habits, attitude, and excuses:

• Do you explain away stress as temporary ("I just have a million things going on right now") even though you can't remember the last time you took a breather?

• Do you define stress as an integral part of your work or home life ("Things are always crazy around here") or as a part of your personality ("I have a lot of nervous energy, that's all").

• Do you blame your stress on other people or outside events, or view it as entirely normal and unexceptional?

Until you accept responsibility for the role you play in creating or maintaining it, your stress level will remain outside your control.

Start a stress journal

A stress journal can help you identify the regular stressors in your life and the way you deal with them. Each time you feel stressed; keep track of it in your journal. As you keep a daily log, you will begin to see patterns and common themes.

Write down:

• What caused your stress (make a guess if you're unsure).

• How you felt, both physically and emotionally.

• How you acted in response.

• What you did to make yourself feel better.

Look at how you currently cope with stress. Think about the ways you currently manage and cope with stress in your life. Your stress journal can help you identify them. Are your coping strategies healthy or unhealthy, helpful or unproductive? Unfortunately, many people cope with stress in ways that compound the problem.

Unhealthy Ways Of Coping With Stress
These coping strategies may temporarily reduce stress, but they cause more damage in the long run:

• Smoking

• Drinking too much

• Overeating or under-eating

• Zoning out for hours in front of the TV or computer

• Withdrawing from friends, family, and activities

• Using pills or drugs to relax

• Sleeping too much

• Procrastinating

• Filling up every minute of the day to avoid facing problems

• Taking out your stress on others (lashing out, angry outbursts, physical violence)

Learning healthier ways to manage stress
There are many healthy ways to manage and cope with stress, but they all require change. You can either change the situation or change your reaction. When deciding which option to choose, it's helpful to think of the four A's: Avoid, Alter, Adapt or Accept.

Change the situation:

• Avoid the stressor.

• Alter the stressor.

Change your reaction:

• Adapt to the stressor.

• Accept the stressor.

Since everyone has a unique response to stress, there is no "one size fits all" solution to managing it. No single method works for everyone or in every situation, so experiment with different techniques and strategies. Focus on what makes you feel calm and in control.

Not all stress can be avoided, and it's not healthy to avoid a situation that needs to be addressed. You may be surprised, however, by the number of stressors in your life that you can eliminate.

• Learn how to say "no" - Know your limits and stick to them. Taking on more than you can handle is a sure-fire recipe for stress.

• Avoid people who stress you out - If someone consistently causes stress in your life and you can't turn the relationship around, limit the amount of time you spend with that person or end the relationship entirely.

• Take control of your environment - If the evening news makes you anxious, turn the TV off. If traffic's got you tense, take a longer but less travelled route.

• Avoid hot-button topics - If you get upset over religion or politics, cross them off your conversation list. If you repeatedly argue about the same subject with the same people, stop bringing it up or excuse yourself when it's the topic of discussion.

• Trim down your to-do list - Analyze your schedule, responsibilities, and daily tasks. If you've got too much on your plate, distinguish between the "shoulds" and the "musts." Drop tasks that aren't truly necessary to the bottom of the list or eliminate them entirely.

Alter The Situation

If you can't avoid a stressful situation, try to alter it. Figure out what you can do to change things so the problem doesn't present itself in the future. Often, this involves changing the way you communicate and operate in your daily life.

• Express your feelings instead of bottling them up. If something or someone is bothering you, communicate your concerns in an open and respectful way. If you don't voice your feelings, resentment will build and the situation will likely remain the same.

• Be willing to compromise. When you ask someone to change their behaviour, be willing to do the same. If you both are willing to bend at least a little, you'll have a good chance of finding a happy middle ground.

• Be more assertive. Don't take a backseat in your own life. Deal with problems head on, doing your best to anticipate and prevent them. If you've got an exam to study for and your chatty roommate just got home, say up front that you only have five minutes to talk.

• Manage your time better. Poor time management can cause a lot of stress. When you're stretched too thin and running behind, it's hard to stay calm and focused. But if you plan ahead and make sure you don't overextend yourself, you can alter the amount of stress you're under.

If you can't change the stressor, change yourself. You can adapt to stressful situations and regain your sense of control by changing your expectations and attitude.

• Reframe problems. Try to view stressful situations from a more positive perspective. Rather than fuming about a traffic jam, look at it as an opportunity to pause and regroup, listen to your favourite radio station, or enjoy some alone time.

• Look at the big picture. Take perspective of the stressful situation. Ask yourself how important it will be in the long run. Will it matter in a month? An year? Is it really worth getting upset over? If the answer is no, focus your time and energy elsewhere.

• Adjust your standards. Perfectionism is a major source of avoidable stress. Stop setting yourself up for failure by demanding perfection. Set reasonable standards for yourself and others, and learn to be okay with "good enough."

• Focus on the positive. When stress is getting you down, take a moment to reflect on all the things you appreciate in your life, including your own positive qualities and gifts. This simple strategy can help you keep things in perspective.

Adjusting Your Attitude

How you think can have a profound effect on your emotional and physical wellbeing. Each time you think a negative thought about yourself, your body reacts as if it were in the throes of a tension-filled situation. If you see good things about yourself, you are more likely to feel good; the reverse is also true. Eliminate words such as "always," "never," "should," and "must." These are telltale marks of self-defeating thoughts.

Accept The Things You Can't Change

Some sources of stress are unavoidable. You can't prevent or change stressors such as the death of a loved one, a serious illness, or a national recession. In such cases, the best way to cope with stress is to accept things as they are. Acceptance may be difficult, but in the long run, it's easier than railing against a situation you can't change.

• Don't try to control the uncontrollable. Many things in life are beyond our control- particularly the behaviour of other people. Rather than stressing out over them, focus on the things you can control such as the way you choose to react to problems.

• Look for the upside. As the saying goes, "What doesn't kill us makes us stronger." When facing major challenges, try to look at them as opportunities for personal growth. If your own poor choices contributed to a stressful situation, reflect on them and learn from your mistakes.

• Share your feelings. Talk to a trusted friend or make an appointment with a therapist. Expressing what you're going through can be very cathartic, even if there's nothing you can do to alter the stressful situation.

• Learn to forgive. Accept the fact that we live in an imperfect world and that people make mistakes. Let go of anger and resentments. Free yourself from negative energy by forgiving and moving on.

Make Time For Fun And Relaxation

Beyond a take-charge approach and a positive attitude, you can reduce stress in your life by nurturing yourself. If you regularly make time for fun and relaxation, you'll be in a better place to handle life's stressors when they inevitably come.

Healthy Ways To Relax And Recharge

• Go for a walk.

• Spend time in nature.

• Call a good friend.

• Sweat out tension with a good workout.

• Write in your journal.

• Take a long bath.

• Light scented candles

- Savor a warm cup of coffee or tea.

- Play with a pet.

- Work in your garden.

- Get a massage.

- Curl up with a good book.

- Listen to music.

- Watch a comedy

Don't get so caught up in the hustle and bustle of life that you forget to take care of your own needs. Nurturing yourself is a necessity, not a luxury.

- Set aside relaxation time. Include rest and relaxation in your daily schedule. Don't allow other obligations to encroach. This is your time to take a break from all responsibilities and recharge your batteries.

- Connect with others. Spend time with positive people who enhance your life. A strong support system will buffer you from the negative effects of stress.

• Do something you enjoy every day. Make time for leisure activities that bring you joy, whether it be stargazing, playing the piano, or working on your bike.

• Keep your sense of humour. This includes the ability to laugh at yourself. The act of laughing helps your body fight stress in a number of ways.

Learn The Relaxation Response

You can control your stress levels with relaxation techniques that evoke the body's relaxation response, a state of restfulness that is the opposite of the stress response. Regularly practicing these techniques will build your physical and emotional resilience, heal your body, and boost your overall feelings of joy and equanimity.

Adopt A Healthy Lifestyle

You can increase your resistance to stress by strengthening your physical health.

• Exercise regularly. Physical activity plays a key role in reducing and preventing the effects of stress. Make time for at least 30 minutes of exercise, three times per week. Nothing beats aerobic exercise for releasing pent-up stress and tension.

• Eat a healthy diet. Well-nourished bodies are better prepared to cope with stress, so be mindful of what you eat. Start your day right with breakfast, and keep your energy up and your mind clear with balanced, nutritious meals throughout the day.

• Reduce caffeine and sugar. The temporary "highs" caffeine and sugar provide often end in with a crash in mood and energy. By reducing the amount of coffee, soft drinks, chocolate, and sugar snacks in your diet, you'll feel more relaxed and you'll sleep better.

• Avoid alcohol, cigarettes, and drugs. Self-medicating with alcohol or drugs may provide an easy escape from stress, but the relief is only temporary. Don't avoid or mask the issue at hand; deal with problems head on and with a clear mind.

• Get enough sleep. Adequate sleep fuels your mind, as well as your body. Feeling tired will increase your stress because it may cause you to think irrationally.

Chapter Five
Anger Mitigation

Life is full with incessant hardships and ease. The dualistic phenomenon of hardship and ease appears in our life, now and then, to make us happy or gloomy, active or passive, defensive or aggressive, realistic or surrealistic. An event/interaction creates three types of sentiments or motivates us towards three types of reactions, it can make us angry or affectionate or indifferent. Angry feelings are developed due to unfavorable situation/person, affectionate sentiments are outcome of some favorable situation/person, and, thirdly, an individual is indifferent towards some un-related situation/person; an unrelated situation has no consequences, positive or negative, on someone's life. A pro-active and moderate attitude is used by normal individuals to handle an upcoming problem or a befallen trouble, on the contrary, a passive or unjust attitude towards some problem/person creates harmful consequences.

Human mind has three psychological powers - perceptual power, emotional power, and will power. A mindset is unique equilibrium of these basic mind powers. We may compare the mind forces' phenomenon with colors' phenomenon. There are three basic colors - yellow, blue, and red. We can get countless colors by combining these basic colors through mixing various proportions of these colors. A change in basic color ultimately changes the final appearance; the same is true about mindset. Any change, qualitative or quantitative, in basic powers changes the overall power structure of mind or changes the mindset. The basic powers are changed due to multiple stimuli. For example, an instinctual desire may distort the equilibrium; a social interaction may disturb the balance, an economic condition can disproportionate the overall stability, and so on and so forth. A Scientific Approach or some Transcendental Guidance is necessary to mange or to avoid the recurrent disturbances. A misbalanced mindset creates inappropriate attitude such as anger or leniency. During anger perceptual power is unable to solve the problems, accurately, emotional power is unable to control her sentiments, courteously, and will power is incapable to mange her intentions, wisely. Anger is, thus, an unjust attitude towards someone or something; it is an abnormal response.

Bases Of Anger (Root Cause Analysis)

A root cause analysis leads us towards better understanding of something. We may group the root causes of anger into two categories - internal as well as external.

Internal Causes:-

We have been endowed by multiple instincts to survive such as parental instinct, sexual instinct, gregarious instinct, and life instinct. The satisfaction of instinctual pressures is necessary for normal life. The very basis of instinctual desires is natural structure of body and mind, i.e., instinctual pressure is not based on learning or experiments. A person can fulfill his natural desire up to indefinite level and may hurt someone during the desire satisfaction activity. Whenever, a satisfaction activity approaches to a hurting point, materially or spiritually, the natural instinctive activity becomes a lust. A lusty behavior is only a human phenomenon. It arises due to power of liberal choices or liberty granted to mankind by Omnipotent. We have four major lusts - lust for pleasure, lust for wealth, lust for power, and lust for fame. Anger is cropped up due to some hurdles/detractors appears during a desire satisfaction journey of instincts. Anger is a negative sentiment because it appears at a point when instinctual desire becomes a lusty behavior, a hurting attitude. A liberal choice must accommodate the rights of others or society at large to develop a responsible personality. A lusty behavior or anger can be controlled through better understanding of liberty-responsibility dualism. A non-lusty person may also behave like angry person due to some haste. During haste an individual try to achieve/rectify something quickly in order to avoid upcoming problems or to mitigate the effects of befallen troubles. The hasty response or quick fixing, generally, leads towards angry sentiments.

Man is a social entity. He cannot live in isolation. He interacts with his fellow human beings. Human interaction has three aspects - social, economic, and political. Moreover, a collective interaction can take two distinct shapes - cooperative and competitive. A competitive interaction is predominantly hostile attitude towards each other; everyone is striving for self rights, obviously, a situation of cutthroat competition. The ultimate outcome of non-healthy or unfair competition is utter loss or corruption; a corrupt situation inevitably leads every one towards some aggressive behavior or anger. A corrupt/unjust society is essentially an angry society. A strong system or effective leadership is required to mange the competition level among individuals/groups within reasonable limits. On the other hand, the cooperative environment creates feeling of love and respect towards each other, consequently affectionate attitude is manifested during multiple and multidimensional interactions. A cooperative society is based on merit and adopts win-win approach towards life issues. It is noteworthy that leniency in attitude during some interaction is not cooperation; it is another shape of corruption.

Anger Management (Long-Run Perspective)

We may understand/explain the anger sentiments and its management under two captions - Controlled Anger and Uncontrolled Anger.

Controlled Anger:-

We are endowed with two natural restraints against negative behavior-patterns of life, they are Intellect and Intuition. Intellect gives a composed, convergent, and concentrated look to one's attitude. However, intellect may diverge during some inferential/generalization activity. There are two restraints on intellect - logic and pragmatism. Logic is tool of reasoning and generalization. A logical behavior is tested weapon against divergent intellectual tendencies. A logically refined intellect is best fence against anger and make it controlled anger. The other restraint on intellect is pragmatism. A pragmatic approach is predominantly wisdom oriented approach; it is practical approach and leads the intellectual effort towards some fruitful solutions for self and others. A pragmatic tendency of an individual puts practical limits on anger. The second restraint on anger is intuition, intuition is a psycho-spiritual entity to discover a generalized truth through some super-logical patterns; it has some transcendental linkages. Intellect is subservient to intuition during multiple intuitive activities of probing, discovering, inventing, and creating. Intellect works through step by step process while intuition unearths the universal truth with some quantum leap. Intuition is a force that makes anger a controllable reaction and put some limits on it and tries to make it beneficial for self and others. Intuition diverts the anger sentiments towards some healthy activities through some emotional attachments. According to religious teachings, a person is brave and courageous if he has control on his angry feelings, an intuitive religious attachment, thus, control anger.

Uncontrolled Anger:-

Uncontrolled anger is harmful for self and others. It is practical shape of anger. It can lead towards some dire and devastating consequences for self and others. During uncontrolled anger physical aspect is disturbed, psychological powers are mutilated and spiritual balance is shattered. Intellect becomes redundant and intuition is unable to work. Uncontrolled anger disturbs, severely, the normal working of heart and brain. These two systems, nervous and circulatory, play a decisive role in one's physical health; other body systems are also disturbed due to malfunctioning of these two basic systems. The physical health is at stake during uncontrolled anger. Moreover, uncontrolled anger disturbs the cooperative ties of social life, demoralize the just economic struggle of economic agents, and detract the egalitarian political struggle of civil society. Uncontrolled anger converts the just and merciful spiritual urges into some inhuman tendencies. An unjust or exaggerated or anger mindset of a genius mind may distort the collective structure of society. For example, two movements of 20th century, Psycho-Analysis and Communism, are outcome of negative or angry approach towards existing structure of collective life. The founders (Marx & Freud) wrongly conceived the basis of exploitative economic system or individual mental disorders in religion or moral structure of prohibition and inhibition, these movements wrongly channeled the anger sentiments of masses against intellect, intuition, religion, and civilization.

Anger Management (Short-Run Perspective)

The best approach to manage anger is to invoke, refine, and develop Intellect and Intuition. It is permanent and long-run approach towards anger management. It makes one's mindset fairly competitive and reasonably cooperative. It gives calm, cool, and sober look to an individual. However, anger is extremely swift phenomenon; generally, it gives no opportunity to a person to activate intellect or intuition, quickly and timely. The general practical strategies/tactics are:

- .Silence,keep silence for a while, most probably the extreme feelings will go down into some normal limits settled by intellect and intuition,
- .Change of Position,person can sit or may walk or may lay down for a while to normalize the reaction,

- Use of Water,person can take water or may wash hand, mouth, etc,

- .Change of Environment,person can leave the hostile environment for some time,

.Self-Suggestion,person can suggest some positive things/sentences or may divert his thoughts towards some positive outcomes of affection or negative consequences of anger.

These strategies / tactics work marvelously to cool down the extreme situations or sentiments.

Levels & Effects Of Affection

Affection or feeling of love towards something / somebody is natural emotion of human being. There are two reasons behind affection - inherent attributes of somebody/something and innate inclinations of an individual towards something/somebody. Whatever may be the cause it gives emotional attachment to someone with something /somebody. Affection has four types or levels - abstract, animate, human and transcendental. At abstract level, we have strong feeling of love towards art work, poetry, and music. At animate level, we love animals/plants such as pets/ trees of various kinds. At human level, we have strong love feelings towards fellow human beings; the human level also gains strength from instinctual tendency of human nature. At transcendental level, we have strong love feelings towards Transcendental Reality / God, it is urging of soul.

Affection creates dual effects on human personality and behavior - active & passive. An active affection is positive and leads towards some contribution towards wellbeing of self or others. A passive affection is impractical and unable to control lethargy, a detrimental situation for self and others. It is noteworthy that a lethargic attitude of a leader/entrepreneur is more detrimental for followers/system than his unjust actions.

Excess / Shortage of everything is bad; the maxim is also valid about affection. Affection may convert into some lenient attitude; it must be managed through some rational guidance and social pressure to avoid leniency. A rational guidance is impulsion, imposed from inside, while the social pressure is compulsion, imposed from outside. It is noteworthy that a lenient attitude is more harmful than angry attitude. A leniency can make someone an unwise friend. It is said an unwise friend is more dreadful than wise enemy. On the contrary, a shortage of affection may tend someone towards some non-reliable/harmful sources of affection. The ultimate outcome of such attitude would be detrimental for both, affection receiver and affection provider.

Chapter Six

Finding Happiness

Most people think of happiness as pure hedonism or instant gratification. The feeling of pleasure you get after eating chocolate, soaking in a warm bath, winning a prize, or having a great glass of wine is short-term happiness. What you really want to strive for in life is long-term pleasure and satisfaction that comes with true happiness. True happiness involves taking an honest view of yourself and the world around you. It leads to discovering what's really meaningful in your life and capitalizing on those virtues. True happiness is values-based yet influenced by your emotions. People who have high emotional intelligence are optimistic, in tune with their passions, and emotionally self-aware, making them hap-pier than people who struggle in these areas. This chapter helps you see the connection between emotional intelligence and happiness, and offers some tools to help you increase your awareness of what can give you real happiness and how to achieve it.

We all know people who see the world through rose-colored glasses. No matter what's going on around them, they see the silver lining. Everything is great. But are they truly happy? Merriam-Webster's Online Dictionary defines happiness as "a state of well-being and contentment" and "a pleasurable or satisfying experience." This definition is pretty open to whether happiness comes from the inside (your experience of the world) or the outside (the outside event itself).

I believe that you create real happiness from within. You might get some short-term happiness from a box of chocolates, but you probably have longer-lasting, more meaningful happiness from working on a project that you're excited about or building a relationship with someone you love. Universal agreement exists, even in non-Westernized societies, that happiness and life satisfaction are important; people everywhere think about happiness often. Studies by happiness-expert psychologist Ed Diener, of the University of Illinois, and his colleagues, who surveyed people around the world, show that only 6 percent of people rate money as more important than happiness. In fact, 69 percent of the people in a worldwide survey rate happiness as the most important thing in their lives.

Understanding The Benefits Of Being Happy

People who feel good see life as an interesting challenge, even when they encounter bumps along the road. Because they feel good, they attract people to them, enlarging their circle of friends. Having more friends gives them more resources when they are in need. When you're in a good mood, you're better positioned to take on challenges. Happy people are more confident, optimistic, likeable, and energetic, and they feel better about themselves. People who feel good for a great deal of the day tend to feel good about their work and home, and they're happier overall about life. In fact, research shows that people who are happier in life are more successful in certain aspects of living. For example, happier people are more successful in marriage, friendships, income, work performance, and health. Many people ask which came first, the happiness or the success. We know definitively that happiness precedes these success experiences. The ability to put yourself in a good mood leads to better enjoyment of work, marriage, home, and health. When you're happy, you simply have a better overall attitude about life. Practicing emotional intelligence provides the skills you need to be able to put yourself in a good mood, even when life isn't going your way.

Changing Your Emotions

You can improve your happiness by taking steps to change your emotions. Now, you don't want to change all your emotions. You simply want to decrease your negative emotions and maintain or augment your positive emotions. One way to sustain positive emotions is to become more aware of what types of thoughts are associated with those emotions. Looking at your positive emotions as a consequence or outcome, try to figure out which thoughts give rise to these feelings. So, for example, if you feel good each time you think about a problem you're trying to solve or the dinner you're planning to cook, you can increase the amount of time you have these kinds of thoughts during the day. You more likely want to change the negative emotions. Use the starting point, the consequence, as your opportunity to identify which of a wide range of emotions you're experiencing. After you identify the emotion that you want less of, you can change the thoughts that lead up to that emotion. Psychologists call this type of emotional change cognitive reappraisal, which means you're developing a new way of looking at your world.

Knowing Your Strengths And Weaknesses

Emotionally intelligent people are self-aware. They know themselves well. They can read their own emotions and know how to manage them. They're also good at knowing their own strengths and weaknesses. An important emotional skill that happy people possess is self-regard. By knowing your strengths and weaknesses, and accepting yourself for who you are, you can deal with challenging issues that you encounter. Building your confidence based on a realistic appraisal of your skills gives you the inner strength to approach situations that you encounter.

The current thinking about happiness suggests that it's a long-term goal and that you can gradually reach a much happier life situation by following a number of exercises. Through specific activities, such as those described below, you can elevate your state of mind, which can affect various aspects of your life success. Martin Seligman, a former President of the American Psychological Association and pioneer of the Positive Psychology movement, outlined a number of aspects of what he calls authentic happiness. According to Seligman, you can experience three types of happiness:

✓ Pleasant life: Pleasures, instant gratification, or hedonism

✓ Good life: Getting the things that you want or desire

✓ Meaningful life: Belonging to and serving in something larger and more worthwhile than just your own pleasures and desires

Authentic happiness combines all three lives and provides for the full life — a life that satisfies all three criteria of happiness. Seligman tried a number of exercises with many people that were designed to increase happiness among the thousands of visitors to his Web sites. Two of the exercises demonstrated a long-term effect, increasing happiness over six months:

✓ Three good things in life: In this exercise, you write down at the end of each day three things that went well for you that day. You also record what caused the good thing to happen. Carry out this exercise for a week. As well as the cause of the thing that went well, write down an explanation of why you think the good thing happened.

✓ Using signature strengths in a new way: In this exercise, people select their "signature" strengths from a list of strengths. These strengths might include social skills, creativity, negotiating, leadership, caring for others, peacemaking, humility, optimism, enthusiasm, fairness, honesty, teamwork, self-control, and so on. Although merely identifying your top five strengths doesn't have much benefit, you can see a long-term benefit by trying to use one of the top five strengths in a new and different way for a week.